SAND CASTLES

SAND CASTLES

A play by Bob Larbey

Based on an idea by Trisha Larbey

AMBER LANE PRESS

All rights whatsoever in this play are strictly reserved and application for professional performance should be made before rehearsals begin to:
The Agency
24 Pottery Lane
Holland Park
London W11 4LZ

Application for amateur performance should be made before rehearsals begin to:
Samuel French Ltd.
52 Fitzroy Street
London W1P 6JR

No performance may be given unless a licence has been obtained.

First published in 2000 by
Amber Lane Press Ltd.
Church Street
Charlbury
Oxford OX7 3PR
Telephone: 01608 810024

Printed and bound by
The Guernsey Press Co. Ltd., Guernsey, C.I.

ISBN: 1 872868 29 0

The action of *Sand Castles* takes place on a beach in the south of England but for regional purposes it can be set anywhere on the coast, and local geographical references may be changed to suit the area where the play is performed.

ACT ONE
Scene 1   A summer morning.
Scene 2   An hour later.

ACT TWO
Scene 1   Early next morning.
Scene 2   The next morning.
Scene 3   The end of the season.

CHARACTERS

WILLIAM PATTERSON
MARGARET PATTERSON (William's wife)

STAN BILLET
BERNICE BILLET (Stan's wife)
MOTHER (Mrs. Billet – Stan's mother)
PAULINE (Bernice's sister)

DOUG
DEBS (Doug's niece)
BECKY (Doug's niece)

MRS. PENFOLD
MRS. NEWMAN
IDA

A BEACHCOMBER

MR. KITE
MRS. KITE

TWO CHILDREN

Sand Castles by Bob Larbey was commissioned specially by BT for its BT Biennial 2000 project, which took place from 14-21 October 2000. The following societies took part:

Abbey Theatre Club, Tayside
Abingdon Drama Club, Oxfordshire
Actors of North Tawton, Devon
Advance Theatre Company, Bedfordshire
Apollo Players, Isle of Wight
Attfield Theatre Company, Shropshire
Bath Operatic and Dramatic Society, Avon
Birchvale Players, Dumfries and Galloway
Blyth Players, Nottinghamshire
Bolton Little Theatre, Greater Manchester
Bovey Tracey Players, Devon
Bramham Drama Group, West Yorkshire
Brampton Theatre Club (Bawds), Cambridgeshire
Broughton Players, Northamptonshire
Carleton Theatre Group, West Yorkshire
Carnon Downs Drama Group, Cornwall
Cherryhill Theatre Company, Kent
Chesil Theatre Company, Hampshire
Conquest Theatre, Hereford and Worcester
Country Players, Bedfordshire
Dee Dankyi Art School, London
Dilys Guite Players Limited, South Yorkshire
Dunlop Players, Strathclyde
Durham Dramatic Society, Durham
Eclipse Theatre School, Greater Manchester
Edward Alderton Theatre, Kent
Exeter Little Theatre Company, Devon
Felixstowe Amateur Dramatic and Operatic Society, Suffolk
Flore Boards, Northamptonshire
Forest Row Dramatic Society, East Sussex
Garden Suburb Theatre, London
Gosforth Amateur Dramatic Society, Cumbria

Goudhurst Amateur Dramatic Society, Kent
Grange Amateur Dramatic Society, Cumbria
Halton Amateur Theatrical Society, Buckinghamshire
Hampton Players, West Midlands
Harlington Performs, Bedfordshire
Hayling Island Amateur Dramatic Society, Hampshire
Highbury Little Theatre, West Midlands
Hillman's Ancient and Modern, Northamptonshire
Honley Players Amateur Dramatic Society, West Yorkshire
Lace Market Theatre, Nottinghamshire
Lindsey Rural Players, Lincolnshire
Millers Amateur Dramatic Society, Kent
Minehead Amateur Dramatic Society, Somerset
Mixed Company, East Sussex
Newmarket Operatic and Dramatic Society, Suffolk
Nonentities Society, Hereford and Worcester
Off Centre Theatre, Gwent
Ostreme Theatre Players, West Glamorgan
Ouse Valley Theatre Company, Bedfordshire
Peters Players, Surrey
Phoenix Players (Portsmouth), Hampshire
Pickwick Theatre, Wiltshire
Rhyl Liberty Players, Clwyd
Rushen Players, Isle of Man
Saltburn 53 Drama Group, Cleveland
Sarisbury Theatre Company, Hampshire
Sawston Players, Cambridgeshire
Saxon Theatre Group, Essex
Schopstone Theatre Company, Derbyshire
SECGA Theatre Company, West Midlands
7/6, Essex
Shawbury Village Players, Shropshire
Shinfield Players Theatre & Arts Centre, Berkshire
South London Theatre, London
St Bernadette's Players, Lancashire
Start Theatre Company, Kent

Stevenage Lytton Players, Hertfordshire
Stoke Climsland Amateur Theatrical Society, Cornwall
Tamaritans Theatre Company, Devon
Teignmouth Players, Devon
The Players, Skelmersdale, Lancashire
Total Arts Community Theatre, Staffordshire
Trencrom Revellers Theatre Club, Cornwall
Wednesday Players, Essex
Wells Operatic Society, Somerset
Weston-Super-Mare Dramatic Society, Avon
Wickhambrook Players, Suffolk
Wilstead Players, Bedfordshire
Windlesham Drama Group, Surrey
Woodley Theatre, Berkshire
Workington Playgoers, Cumbria

ACT ONE

Scene 1

A summer morning.

The stage is taken up by three beach huts forming a slight arc. Each hut is about the size of a decent garden shed, with a door and two little windows. The two end huts are neatly painted but the middle hut is less pristine in appearance. NB: In the interest of saving space there is no need to be able to see right into the back of the huts when the doors are open. The interiors are fairly dim anyway, so all we need to see are any little bits of furniture or effects near the front.

The light is bright. Sound effects of distant beach noises, which should fade under. The backcloth is of sand dunes and hummocks of tufted grass.

The doors of the middle and S/L huts are closed and padlocked. The door of the S/R hut is ajar. Outside this hut two folding chairs and a little table are set up. On the table are a knitting basket, a novel, a copy of The Times *and a pair of binoculars.*

WILLIAM PATTERSON *comes out of the S/R hut. He is in his sixties, upper-class, and wears a panama hat, a discreet sports shirt, long shorts, socks to just below the knee and heavy brown sandals. He breathes in the warm air then takes up the binoculars, loops them around his neck, puts them to his eyes and looks out to sea. He fixes on a spot then calls back into the hut.*

WILLIAM: Margaret!

MARGARET: [*off*] Yes?

WILLIAM: There's a small child drifting out to sea on a rubber shark.

MARGARET: [*off*] A rubber what?

WILLIAM: Shark!

> [MARGARET PATTERSON *comes out of the hut. She is about the same age as* WILLIAM *and wears a Liberty-print dress, straw hat and sandals.*]

MARGARET: How big is it?

WILLIAM: About six feet long, I suppose.

MARGARET: I meant the child.

WILLIAM: Oh. Hard to say – toddlerish, I suppose. Here, see for yourself.

> [*He goes to take the binoculars from around his neck but* MARGARET *tries to look through them before he can do so.*]

Just a minute, just a minute!

> [*He takes off his hat, unloops the strap of the binoculars and gives them to her.*]

You always did dash at things.

MARGARET: What about the SAS?

WILLIAM: What *about* the SAS?

MARGARET: Well, they don't do badly, and that's their motto: 'Who Dashes Wins'.

> [WILLIAM *doesn't look too sure about this as* MARGARET *looks through the binoculars.*]

All I can see is blue.

WILLIAM: You're looking at the sky! Down a bit. [*helping her*] A bit more. That's about it. Now what have you got?

MARGARET: A man falling off his surfboard.

WILLIAM: Oh, let me have a look.

[*Forgetting his own advice,* WILLIAM *looks through the binoculars without unlooping the strap from around* MARGARET's *neck.*]

MARGARET: Who's dashing now?

WILLIAM: I'm just trying to get you aligned. Now, find the fellow with the surfboard – he's trying to get back on now – and then go directly left from him for about fifty yards.

[MARGARET *looks through the binoculars again.*]

MARGARET: Got him! He's back on. No he's not, he's fallen in again.

WILLIAM: Fifty yards to the left!

[MARGARET *swivels the binoculars to the left but as she does so a* BEACHCOMBER *enters* S/R. *He is wearing army surplus fatigues and carries a metal detector. He is wearing earphones and, intent on his 'sweeps', he blocks* MARGARET's *view completely.*]

MARGARET: Now I can't see anything at all!

WILLIAM: Of course you can't.

[*He taps the* BEACHCOMBER *on the shoulder.*]

Excuse me.

[*The* BEACHCOMBER *just nods pleasantly, so* WILLIAM *lifts one of his earphones.*]

Excuse me!

[*The* BEACHCOMBER *takes off his earphones.*]

BEACHCOMBER: Oh, sorry. Can I help you?

WILLIAM: We're trying to spot a toddler drifting out to sea on a rubber shark.

BEACHCOMBER: Where? Where?

[*Now the* BEACHCOMBER *tries to look through the binoculars without unlooping the strap from* MARGARET's *neck.*]

MARGARET: William!

> [WILLIAM *slaps the* BEACHCOMBER*'s hands away.*]

WILLIAM: Will you stop that! It's spreading like the Plague, this habit. Now Margaret, will you give me the glasses please? I'm sure I've got a fix on things now.

> [MARGARET *unloops the binoculars and hands them to* WILLIAM, *who looks through them.*]

Now where's that fool of a windsurfer gone?

BEACHCOMBER: Do you think we should raise the alarm?

MARGARET: [*looking around*] What alarm?

BEACHCOMBER: It would be the Coastguard, wouldn't it?

WILLIAM: My God, what a pair of thighs!

MARGARET: William, you're supposed to be looking for a toddler on a rubber shark.

WILLIAM: Oh, I found him all right. So has his mother. They could crush coconuts, thighs like that.

BEACHCOMBER: I could have dashed up to the phone box.

WILLIAM: Why?

BEACHCOMBER: To alert the Coastguard. Well, somebody had to do something.

MARGARET: You didn't do anything.

BEACHCOMBER: I was ready to. I was about to. I was poised.

WILLIAM: Look here, this is all academic anyway. There wasn't an emergency. There never is. Over the years we must have seen dozens of children drifting out to sea on various rubber things and somebody always retrieves them.

BEACHCOMBER: There's always a first time.

WILLIAM: That's very true.

BEACHCOMBER: Yes, there's always a first time.

WILLIAM: Sometimes a second.

BEACHCOMBER: [*missing the sarcasm*] And sometimes a second.

MARGARET: Would you excuse me?

[*She goes into the hut.*]

BEACHCOMBER: Well, I must be on my merry way.

WILLIAM: What exactly do you look for with that thing?

BEACHCOMBER: Who's to say? It could be anything.

WILLIAM: Anything metal presumably?

BEACHCOMBER: Oh, yes, it would have to be metal. 'Over the years,' you said?

WILLIAM: Donkeys. My wife and I retired down here a while back and bought the beach hut then. Good investment – decent base.

BEACHCOMBER: I don't have a base. It's all wanderlust with me.

WILLIAM: Well, you're young enough to do that. See the world while you can.

BEACHCOMBER: Oh, not the world. I don't do the world. But the south coast – anywhere! In the holidays, of course.

WILLIAM: That's wanderlust for you.

[*Again missing the sarcasm, the* BEACHCOMBER *nods sagely.*]

BEACHCOMBER: Well, nice talking to you. I must be on my merry way.

WILLIAM: Good hunting.

BEACHCOMBER: Thank you. You know, it sounds silly, but I almost hope that I never do find buried treasure. It's the thrill of the chase that's the thing – the thrill of the chase!

[*He adjusts his earphones and exits* S/L, *making his 'sweeps' as he goes.* WILLIAM *watches him.*]

WILLIAM: The thrill of the chase.

[MARGARET *comes out of the hut carrying a tray with tea-things on it. She sets it down on the table.*]

MARGARET: I was quite wrong, you know.

WILLIAM: If you mean my proposal of marriage, don't you think
            it's a bit late in the day?

MARGARET: About the SAS. Their motto isn't 'Who Dashes Wins',
            it's 'Who Dares Wins'.

WILLIAM: I thought 'Dashes' sounded wrong.

            [*They sit at the table and* MARGARET *pours the
            tea.*]

            Aren't we a little early? It's only a quarter to.

MARGARET: I thought we'd defy convention.

WILLIAM: Talking of convention, the Billet family should arrive
            today.

MARGARET: Yes.

WILLIAM: That wasn't a very enthusiastic 'yes'.

MARGARET: Oh, they're basically nice people. It's just . . . you
            know.

WILLIAM: Yes. *Did* you ever regret accepting my proposal?

MARGARET: What a strange question.

WILLIAM: Yes, but did you?

MARGARET: Not for one minute.

            [WILLIAM *reaches across the table and takes her
            hand, then they both sit back to drink their tea.*]

            Mother did.

WILLIAM: She never took to me, your mother.

MARGARET: She thought you were feckless.

WILLIAM: Feckless? Why?

MARGARET: You used to wear rather gaudy ties.

            [WILLIAM *considers this for a moment but can
            make no sense of it. He has another look through
            the binoculars.*]

            Are you looking for those thighs again?

WILLIAM: No, just the heaving mass of humanity down on the beach. Why do women always scream when they run into the sea?

MARGARET: Actually, it's quite therapeutic to have a good scream.

WILLIAM: Go ahead and have one now if you like.

MARGARET: One doesn't scream to order.

WILLIAM:.   Kilts.

MARGARET: What about kilts?

WILLIAM: They always seem to make women scream.

MARGARET: That would be kilts on a windy day, would it?

WILLIAM: Oh, yes, wind is essential.

MARGARET: Well, there aren't likely to be any kilts on the beach, so I don't think I shall be screaming.

WILLIAM: Fair enough.

                       [*He gets up and looks at the middle hut.*]

                       I wonder what happened to the Woodersons. That's three seasons in a row they haven't turned up.

MARGARET: They didn't say anything the last time we saw them.

WILLIAM: Perhaps they didn't know.

MARGARET: Didn't know what?

WILLIAM: Whatever the set of circumstances were that would prevent them coming for the next three years.

MARGARET: Oh, I see, yes.

                       [*She gets up and joins* WILLIAM. *They find themselves trying to peer in through the net-curtained windows.*]

WILLIAM: Why are we doing this?

MARGARET: I'm not sure really.

                       [*She tries the padlock.*]

WILLIAM: Why did you do that?

MARGARET: I'm not really sure of that either. It's your fault for making me curious.

WILLIAM: I simply posed a question.

MARGARET: If you were Hercules Poirot. the Woodersons' bodies
              would be lying on the floor in there.

WILLIAM: Which makes me very glad I'm not Hercules Poirot.

              [*They wander back towards their chairs as a mid-
              dle-aged woman,* MRS. PENFOLD, *enters* S/L. *She
              carries the spool of a kite with only the string
              dangling from it.* MRS. PENFOLD *is a woman with
              a chip or two on her shoulder.*]

MRS. P: Have you seen a kite?

MARGARET: [*not liking her tone*] Dozens.

MRS. P: [*pointing to the string*] I meant this one.

MARGARET: There isn't a kite there at all.

MRS. P: The kite that used to be there!

MARGARET: [*to* WILLIAM] Have you seen the kite that used to be
              there?

WILLIAM: Sorry – can't help.

MRS. P: Junk. that's what they sell in that shop in the village.
              junk! A small fortune I paid for that kite and it's no
              sooner in the air than the string breaks. I've got the
              kids howling and of course he does nothing. He just
              lies there in his thong.

WILLIAM: Are you sure it came up this way?

MRS. P: Of course I'm sure. 'There it goes.' I said. 'up the posh
              bit.'

WILLIAM: The posh bit?

MRS. P: That's what we call the beach hut bit – the posh bit.
              You sit up here with your tables – proper cups and
              saucers. You look down on the rest of us.

WILLIAM: That's only a matter of topography.

MRS. P: In other words. class.

WILLIAM: No. in other words. local geography. This area is
              simply higher than the beach.

MARGARET: So, physically speaking, we do look down on you.

MRS. P: I'm talking mentally.

MARGARET: Yes, I rather think you are.

[*The two women look daggers at each other.*]

WILLIAM: [*quickly*] I'm sorry we couldn't help you with the kite.

MRS. P: And I'm sorry to have dared set foot on your private piece of property.

WILLIAM: The only private property we have here is the beach hut.

MRS. P: Not the sand?

WILLIAM: Of course not the sand.

MRS. P: So anyone could sit here if they wanted to? I could sit here if I wanted to?

WILLIAM: If you wanted to, yes.

MRS. P: [*to* MARGARET] You're worried now, aren't you?

MARGARET: I've brought the wrong book out.

[*She goes into the hut.*]

MRS. P: She's shaking in her shoes.

WILLIAM: I've never seen Margaret shake in anything.

MRS. P: That's what they said about Marie Antoinette.

WILLIAM: Did they really? I didn't know that.

MRS. P: Well they did – in so many words. Anyway, I've got that kite to find.

WILLIAM: Good luck.

MRS. P: Luck? Luck and the Penfold family are total strangers!

[MRS. PENFOLD *exits* S/R *as* MARGARET *comes back out of the hut with her book.*]

MARGARET: What a dreadful woman.

WILLIAM: I think she may be setting up a guillotine on the beach later.

[MARGARET *sits at the table and opens her book.* WILLIAM *looks at the middle hut.*]

Nice people, the Woodersons – quiet people.

> [MARGARET *doesn't answer and* WILLIAM *feels some tension coming from her.*]

Is something the matter?

MARGARET: I do wish you'd told that woman that we *did* own the sand.

WILLIAM: The whole beach?

MARGARET: Of course not. Just our bit.

WILLIAM: Margaret, we don't have a 'bit'.

MARGARET: But most people on the beach assume we do. Why disabuse them?

WILLIAM: It's not the sort of thing Denis Compton would have done.

MARGARET: He was a cricketer. How do you know he even had a beach hut?

WILLIAM: I don't. It's simply a question of playing life with a straight bat.

> [*He plays an imaginary cricket stroke.*]

STAN: [*off*] Howzat!

> [STAN BILLET *trots on* S/L, *tossing an imaginary cricket ball up in triumph.* STAN *is in his forties, a middle-class would-be achiever. He is wearing jazzy shorts and a T-shirt with some silly slogan printed on it.*]

Here we are again! Different year, same day. How very nice to see you again, Mr. and Mrs. Patterson.

WILLIAM: Look here, you must call us William and Margaret. We have been meeting each other for six years now.

> [STAN, *clearly a little in awe of them, takes this as an honour.*]

STAN: That's really first-class of you. And you must call me Stan.

MARGARET: Nice to see you again – Stan.

STAN: Do you know what they say about me in the show-room? 'Old Stan never stands still!' [*chuckling*] I always chuckle at that. 'Stan' and 'stands', you see. It's a play on words.

[WILLIAM *sits down.*]

WILLIAM: Isn't your wife with you?

STAN: Bernice? Oh, yes. She and Mother are unloading the Range Rover in the car park. Incidentally, if you ever lean towards a 4x4, I'm your man. Stan's the man.

WILLIAM: I think we're quite happy with the old banger.

STAN: Up to you – your prerogative entirely, Mr. . . . er, William. Incidentally, we've brought the wife's sister with us this year. A bit of a recuperation for her.

MARGARET: Oh dear. Has she been ill?

STAN: Not exactly ill – not in the medical sense. It's a woman thing – you'd understand that.

[MARGARET *doesn't see why she should but* STAN *presses on, flinging his arms wide and taking deep breaths.*]

Smell that air! Say what you like, but this place knocks spots off Barbados!

[*He now launches himself into press-ups. He only manages two and a half, then struggles to his feet, breathing heavily and patting his stomach.*]

Whoops! Too many business lunches in there, I'm afraid. Still, a few weeks on the beach and the old muscle tone will re-assert itself.

[WILLIAM *and* MARGARET *exchange smiles. There obviously never has been any muscle tone.* MR. KITE, *holding a kite spool with the string trailing behind him, trots on* S/R.]

MR. KITE: Let it go! Let it go!

MRS. KITE: [*off*] You're too close!

[MRS. KITE *enters, on the run as well, holding a kite above her head.*]

MR. KITE: Let it go! Let it go!

MRS. KITE: Oh. suit yourself!

[*She releases the kite, which simply flops to the ground.*]

Well, go on – run! Run!

[MR. KITE *does, but the kite simply bumps along behind him.* MRS. KITE *follows, flapping her arms as if to will the kite into the air. They exit* S/L. STAN *looks disapprovingly after them.*]

STAN: A bit far up the beach, weren't they?

MARGARET: That's the third time this morning. We've already had an obnoxious woman and a man with a mine detector.

[STAN *freezes on the spot.*]

STAN: A mine detector? Oh, my God!

WILLIAM: Margaret means a metal detector.

STAN: Oh, sighs of relief all round then. What about this woman?

MARGARET: Yes – a chip on her shoulder.

STAN: Oh, I know the type. It's beach hut envy. There are plenty of them down there. you know. I just wish they'd stay down there.

[*But he brightens as he produces the key to his padlock.*]

Open Sesame!

[*He unlocks the padlock and opens the door to the* S/L *hut.*]

Hello, old friend.

WILLIAM: We were wondering what's happened to the Woodersons.

STAN: [*gravely*] I don't think we shall be seeing the Woodersons again.

WILLIAM: Oh dear.

MARGARET: They haven't died, have they?

STAN: It's rather worse than that.

[*He points dramatically at the middle hut.*]

They've rented!

MARGARET: Rented?

WILLIAM: How do you know?

STAN: We stopped off at the village shop for some milk and there in the window – as plain as the nose on your face – was the card. 'Beach hut for rent'. A photograph was attached and of course I recognized it immediately.

MARGARET: Oh dear.

STAN: Oh dear indeed. I had a lot of time for the Woodersons but I'm afraid they've stabbed us in the back.

[*From* S/L *enter* STAN's *wife*, BERNICE, *her sister*, PAULINE, *and* STAN's *mother* (MOTHER). BERNICE *is in her early forties, always somewhat overdressed.* PAULINE *is some years younger, quietly attractive, but shy, and a little nervous in her movements.* MOTHER *is a miserable old trout, whose clothes make no concession to the weather. She even carries an umbrella.* BERNICE *and* PAULINE *are wearing summer dresses and are loaded down with various items of beach hut paraphernalia.*]

BERNICE: 'I'll open up and be straight back to give you a hand,' you said!

STAN: Sorry, Bernice, I was just . . .

[*But* BERNICE *drops her load and goes to greet* WILLIAM *and* MARGARET.]

BERNICE: Mr. and Mrs. Patterson! How are you both?

MARGARET: Quite well, thank you.

WILLIAM: Oh, and we've decided it's time for Christian names.
             It's William and Margaret.

BERNICE: Oh, how very social. Bernice. And that's my sister,
             Pauline.

             [WILLIAM *and* MARGARET *do little waves.*]

MARGARET: Hello.

WILLIAM: Hello.

PAULINE: Hello.

BERNICE: Put the stuff down, Pauline. Don't stand there like a
             packhorse. Mother, of course, you've already met.

MARGARET: William and Margaret.

MOTHER: Mrs. Billet. [*to* STAN] Am I supposed to stand here all
             day with my legs?

             [STAN *goes into his hut.*]

BERNICE: Stan, get your mother a chair.

             [STAN *re-emerges with a folding chair.*]

STAN: Doing so, my love, doing so.

             [*He unfolds the chair and sets it down.*]

             There we are, Mother. How's that?

MOTHER: Five more minutes and my ankles would have gone
             through the roof.

             [*She sits down, clutching her umbrella and look-
             ing as though she may never move again.* STAN
             looks at the stuff they have brought with them.]

STAN: Where's the rest of the stuff?

BERNICE: In the Range Rover, where do you think?

PAULINE: I'll go.

BERNICE: No you won't. Stan!

STAN: I'm going, I'm going!

[He hurries off S/L. PAULINE picks up some of the baggage.]

BERNICE: What are you doing?

PAULINE: I thought I'd put some of the stuff in the hut.

BERNICE: There's no point, Stan will only have it all out again. He has to put it in in his own particular order.

PAULINE: Well, could we at least get changed? I'm ever so hot.

MOTHER: I'm not.

BERNICE: No harm in that, I suppose – but only bring your little bag.

[BERNICE and PAULINE each pick up a small bag and go towards their hut.]

[to WILLIAM and MARGARET] See you anon!

[PAULINE and BERNICE go into their hut and BERNICE closes the door behind them. STAN enters S/L.]

STAN: Nobody gave me the car keys. *[opening the door of his hut]* I said, nobody . . .

[There is a shriek from PAULINE. STAN jumps back.]

Sorry! Sorry!

[BERNICE pokes her head out.]

BERNICE: What do you think you're playing at?

STAN: I forgot we had her with us.

BERNICE: Well, you'd better start remembering or we shall have incidents. *[handing him the car keys]* There.

STAN: *[calling]* Sorry, Pauline.

[He makes a 'whoops' face at WILLIAM and MARGARET and exits S/L. BERNICE shakes her head and closes the door of the hut behind her. MOTHER stares resolutely ahead.]

MOTHER: They'll all look like boiled lobsters by the end of the day, you mark my words.

MARGARET: [*looking up from her book*] Sorry?

MOTHER: You mark my words.

           [*There is no answer to this so* MARGARET *goes
           back to her book.* WILLIAM *picks up* The Times.]

           Ra!

           [WILLIAM *tries this time.*]

WILLIAM: I beg your pardon?

MOTHER: Ra. He was the ancient Egyptian god of the sun.

WILLIAM: So he was.

MOTHER: I know.

           [*She offers nothing else so* WILLIAM *goes back to
           his newspaper.* BERNICE *comes out of the hut
           wearing a violently coloured swimsuit and sarong
           and a huge straw hat.*]

BERNICE: Something to drink, Mother? I've stocked the cool-
           bag.

MOTHER: Not yet, no. Once I start I'll be up and down to those
           toilets like a thing possessed.

BERNICE: What about you, William and Margaret? May I offer
           you something – sparkling white wine?

MARGARET: Thanks all the same, we've just had tea.

BERNICE: Pauline? Sparkling white wine?

           [PAULINE *comes out of the hut wearing a towel-
           ling robe over a swimsuit.*]

PAULINE: Just mineral water, please. It's a bit early.

BERNICE: Implying?

PAULINE: Nothing – nothing at all.

BERNICE: It's just me then. [*rummaging in the cool-bag*] Where's
           the bottle-opener? [*looking up at* PAULINE] Have you
           got that bikini on under there?

           [*The word 'bikini' makes* WILLIAM *lean forward.*
           MARGARET *pushes him back.*]

PAULINE: No I haven't. I don't know why you made me buy it.

BERNICE: Pauline, I did not *make* you buy it. I just thought you'd look nice in it – more outgoing.

PAULINE: It's too skimpy.

BERNICE: Of course it's not. Wear them while you've still got your figure, that's what I say.

WILLIAM: Hear hear!

MARGARET: William!

BERNICE: You won't attract a man all swaddled up like that.

PAULINE: I don't want to attract anybody. I just want a rest.

BERNICE: Oh, suit yourself. There you are.

> [*She gives* PAULINE *a little bottle of mineral water and a plastic cup, then rummages in the cool-bag again.*]

Where is that bottle-opener?

> [PAULINE *sits on the sand. She does not look very happy.* BERNICE *looks at her and* MOTHER *and sighs, then rummages again.* STAN *enters* S/L, *carrying the rest of the baggage.*]

STAN: There's some fool trying to pitch a tent in the car park.

BERNICE: Where's the bottle-opener?

STAN: Have you tried my 'Bits and Pieces' tin?

BERNICE: Where's your 'Bits and Pieces' tin?

STAN: It's obvious. In the 'Bits and Pieces' bag!

PAULINE: I'll get it.

STAN: You don't know where to look, Pauline.

> [*He selects a bag from the pile.*]

'Bits and Pieces' bag.

> [*He looks in the bag and triumphantly produces a tin.*]

'Bits and Pieces' tin!

BERNICE:	Oh, stop acting like a conjuror, Stan, just give me the bottle-opener.
STAN:	Aren't we a touch early? The sun's not over the yard-arm yet.
	[BERNICE *snatches the bottle-opener and starts to open a bottle of sparkling white wine.*]
BERNICE:	You don't even know what that means.
STAN:	I do. It's a naval expression. It means . . .
MOTHER:	The Dave Clark Five!
STAN:	Pardon, Mother?
MOTHER:	The Dave Clark Five! They made a record called 'Bits and Pieces'.
STAN:	So they did.
MOTHER:	I know. [*singing*] 'Bits and pieces, bits and pieces.'
	[*That's all she sings.*]
BERNICE:	[*to* WILLIAM *and* MARGARET] She drifts in and out these days. [*pouring herself a glass of wine*] No one else then? Cheers!
	[STAN *claps his hands enthusiastically.*]
STAN:	Right then, time to stow the old gear!
	[PAULINE *goes to get up.*]
PAULINE:	I'll help.
STAN:	No, no. I'd sooner do it in my own funny little way.
	[PAULINE *sits down again.*]
BERNICE:	Told you. [*to* STAN] Do you think we could have something to sit on in your own funny little way?
STAN:	That is on my agenda, Bernice.
	[*He begins a series of going into his hut with pieces of baggage and coming out again with three folding chairs.*]
	Incidentally, Mother, I've brought the camp cot in case you fancy a nap later.

MOTHER:	I don't want a nap.
STAN:	You might later.
MOTHER:	Well, I don't want one now.
STAN:	No, all right.

[BERNICE sits in one of the chairs, drink in hand and bottle nearby.]

BERNICE: *[to PAULINE]* You will be taking off that robe at some time, won't you?

PAULINE: Probably.

BERNICE: I mean, if you don't put the goods in the shop window . . .

PAULINE: Oh, Bernice, please!

[BERNICE just 'tuts' and tops up her glass.]

STAN: Well, call me a fool! I've forgotten the foot-pump for the inflatables.

BERNICE: You'll just have to blow them up by hand then.

STAN: That will take hours! Er, excuse me, Mr. . . . . William, I don't suppose you have a foot-pump?

WILLIAM: Sorry, we don't use inflatables any more.

MARGARET: We had a large duck when the boys were young. We called him 'Ducky'.

STAN: Did you really?

WILLIAM: What about that compressed air gadget at the garage?

STAN: No, strictly *verboten*, I'm afraid. They had a nasty explosion with a Loch Ness Monster a few years ago and that was that. Still, never mind, I'll get round to it. 'Where there's a will there's a way', as Shakespeare said to Ann Hathaway!

[He laughs at his own joke. Nobody else does so he gets on. MR. and MRS. KITE cross the stage again. This time she holds the spool and he holds the kite.]

MR. KITE: Faster, faster!

MRS. KITE: Hold it higher!

MR. KITE: I'm not a giant!

MRS. KITE: Right, let go now. Let go now!

MR. KITE: I can't.

MRS. KITE: Why not?

MR. KITE: I've got my finger caught!

MRS. KITE: Oh, you are a fool!

              [*But she keeps on running anyway.*]

MR. KITE: Well, stop running then! Tracey, will you stop?

              [*They go off. The beach-hutters have watched this charade.*]

STAN: [*shouting after them*] Have a care, do! You could have taken my mother's head clean off! [*to* WILLIAM *and* MARGARET] Do you think they're doing it deliberately?

WILLIAM: Well, in fairness, it is higher ground.

STAN: But what about Mother's head?

MOTHER: There's nothing wrong with my head.

STAN: There *could* have been, Mother.

WILLIAM: Safer than the beach, though. Lots of people down there – a far greater risk of decapitation.

STAN: Nevertheless, this all smacks of deliberate encroachment.

MARGARET: I keep thinking about that woman.

STAN: The obnoxious one?

MARGARET: Yes.

STAN: May I join you?

MARGARET: Please do.

              [STAN *gets a chair and moves over to join them.*]

STAN: Tell me, to what lengths did her obnoxiousicity extend?

MARGARET: Politically, far to the left, I'm afraid.

STAN: Oh, good heavens!

MARGARET: She displayed a very keen interest in finding out whether this part was private property or not.

STAN: You didn't tell her?

WILLIAM: I'm afraid I did.

STAN: Oh dear, oh dear.

WILLIAM: Well, one can't actually lie about it, can one?

STAN: Not lie, no. One can waffle a bit, though. If someone says to me, 'Is this part actually private?' I don't lie as such. I just say something like, 'Well, what do you think, with the beach huts and everything?' and that always persuades them that it must be.

WILLIAM: Well, I'm afraid I'm not that subtle.

STAN: No, well, working in the motor trade does develop subtlety as a skill, I suppose.

MARGARET: It's simply a question of respect for other people's space.

STAN: Precisely. Now when I moved my chair over here, I didn't just trample into your space, did I? 'May I?' I said.

MARGARET: As one does.

STAN: Absolutely.

[*Increasingly bored with this,* PAULINE *gets up.*]

PAULINE: I think I'll go for a walk. Excuse me.

[*She exits* S/R.]

BERNICE: Sorry about her.

WILLIAM: Oh, you mustn't apologize. She seems a perfectly nice girl.

BERNICE: Yes, but she won't come out of herself. Swine of a man!

MARGARET: Who is?

BERNICE: Rex Elphinstone. He's the reason she won't come out of herself.

MARGARET: Oh, I see, yes.

> [STAN *looks off* S/L.]

STAN: [*out of the corner of his mouth*] Watch it! Watch it!

> [*A middle-aged northern woman,* IDA, *enters* S/L. *She is carrying a beach bag and a towel and is obviously looking for somewhere to sit.*]

IDA: How do?

> [*Muttered 'good mornings' from the others. They will her to keep going but she puts her towel down in what they consider to be part of their beach huts' space.*]

Nice up here, isn't it?

> [*Muttered agreement from the others.*]

Nice view from higher up.

> [*More muttered agreement from the others.* IDA *sits on her towel. The others look at each other.* IDA *is not a welcome visitor but who is to tell her so? Gestures indicate that* STAN *is elected.* STAN *clears his throat and coughs to attract* IDA*'s attention. She takes no notice so he tries again – louder.*]

Our Quentin had a cough like that, that's why he gave up the fags. Mind you, he was dead a week later – run over by a lorry.

> [*There is no response to this from the others, just fidgety movements, which* IDA *does pick up on.*]

Look, is something wrong?

STAN: Well, it's a question of location.

IDA: What location?

STAN: Yours, actually.

IDA: Oh, I'm from Blackburn.

BERNICE: My husband means your location here.

IDA: A B & B in the village.

BERNICE: No – *here*.

                [*She makes vague perimeter gestures.*]

IDA: I'm sorry, I don't follow.

                [STAN *makes the same gestures only bigger.*]

           No, I'm not with you at all.

MARGARET: We own these beach huts, you see.

IDA: And very nice too.

STAN: [*making the gestures again*] So consequently . . .

IDA: Oh, I see! You're saying that you own the ground in front of them too?

WILLIAM: Well, actually . . .

MARGARET: [*quickly*] Actually . . .

BERNICE: Stan?

STAN: Oh. Well, it's not a point we like to labour but, as you see, with the beach huts and everything . . .

                [*Fortunately for* STAN, IDA *falls for this and gets up, picking up her towel and bag.*]

IDA: Oh, of course, I do apologize. I mean, when you put it like that, it's screamingly obvious, isn't it?

STAN: Not that we labour the point.

IDA: Oh, no, you were most discreet. I'll move further down.

STAN: Thank you very much.

IDA: Sorry to have imposed.

                [*She starts to leave, passing* MOTHER *on the way.*]

MOTHER: Blue and white halves.

IDA: You what, love?

MOTHER: Blackburn Rovers' colours – blue and white halves.

IDA: So they are.

MOTHER: I know.

                [IDA *exits* S/L.]

MARGARET: Well done, Stan – very well done.

STAN: [*preening*] Not bad, was it?

BERNICE: She went off like a lamb.

            [*They wait for* WILLIAM*'s approval but he looks
            doubtful.*]

MARGARET: What?

WILLIAM: Well, I don't want to be a damp squib, but . . .

MARGARET: But *what*, William?

WILLIAM: As Bernice said, 'like a lamb'. But what of others? Our
            fictitious claim to this area actually holds no water
            at all. It is, when all's said and done, just waffle.

            [*The others take this in, depressed by* WILLIAM*'s
            shower of cold water.*]

BERNICE: May I?

MARGARET: Of course.

            [BERNICE *takes her chair over to sit with them.
            Silence falls for a moment. Unnoticed,* MOTHER
            gets up and wanders off S/L.]

STAN: Drip, drip, drip!

BERNICE: Oh, don't be hard on yourself.

STAN: ·I'm not calling myself a drip, Bernice.

BERNICE: Who then?

STAN: All of them! All of them down there!

WILLIAM: Isn't that a bit harsh?

STAN: Not to my way of thinking. Little by little they're erod-
            ing our little world up here. Drip, drip, drip!

WILLIAM: Well, I don't see what we can do about it, apart from
            digging a slit trench and mounting a couple of ma-
            chine-guns.

MARGARET: It isn't funny, William.

BERNICE: It's the politics of resentment, that's what it is.

WILLIAM: Well, I don't think we should make too much of this. We're making them sound like the Huns at the gates of Rome.

STAN: Well, they are in my book!

WILLIAM: Oh, come on, cheer up. Perhaps it's just been a bad day for your Huns. We may not see another one for weeks.

> [WILLIAM *has tempted fate as* MRS. NEWMAN *enters* S/R *with two* CHILDREN.]

MRS. N: Excuse me, do you think the children could use your toilet?

STAN: We don't have toilets.

MRS. N: You must have.

STAN: We do not!

MRS. N: What do you do then?

WILLIAM: Exercise very strict bladder control.

MRS. N: I don't believe you. [*trying to peer into the huts*] You must have toilets!

MARGARET: Would you kindly stop peering into our beach huts?

BERNICE: There are public facilities just up by the Beach Cafe.

MRS. N: In other words, you have got toilets but you're just too mean to let anybody else use them?

STAN: All right, I've had enough of this!

> [*He gets up and points into his hut.*]

There you are, see for yourself! Do you see anything resembling a toilet in there?

MRS. N: They're round the back then.

STAN: They are not! Now clear off!

MRS. N: If my Basil was down here with us, I'd get him to punch your lights out!

> [*The* CHILDREN *whisper urgently in her ear.*]

All right, all right! Come on!

[*She exits* S/L *with the* CHILDREN.]

STAN: Well, that's wonderful, isn't it? I am now being threatened with violence for not having a toilet!

WILLIAM: You were rather rude.

MARGARET: You mustn't let them drag you down to their level.

BERNICE: She wasn't the woman who caused trouble earlier, was she?

MARGARET: No.

STAN: So that's three of them in one morning. They're everywhere!

[*This produces an air of gloom.*]

BERNICE: Oh dear.

STAN: What?

BERNICE: There's something else to worry about.

STAN: There can't be . . .

BERNICE: There is. What kind of people have rented the middle hut?

STAN: Oh God!

WILLIAM: There is one other thing.

MARGARET: What other thing?

WILLIAM: I've only just realized. Stan's mother seems to have disappeared.

[*Everyone looks alarmed.* STAN *lets out a low moan and buries his head in his hands.*]

END OF SCENE 1

Scene 2

An hour later.

Only WILLIAM *is on stage. He sits in his chair, scanning the beach with his binoculars.* PAULINE, *back from her walk, enters* S/L.

PAULINE: Where is everybody?

WILLIAM: I'm afraid Mrs Billet wandered off, so Stan organized a search-party.

PAULINE: Oh Lord!

WILLIAM: Oh, I shouldn't worry. She'll be easy to find. There can't be too many people on the beach with an overcoat and umbrella.

PAULINE: No, I meant Stan organizing something. He tends to get people's backs up when he organizes something.

WILLIAM: Yes, I can see how that might happen. [*apologetically*] I would have joined the search but the old legs don't carry me too far these days.

PAULINE: Why?

WILLIAM: That's a very blunt question.

PAULINE: I'm sorry. I'm not usually blunt at all.

WILLIAM: Oh, don't apologize. There's nothing wrong with a bit of bluntness now and then. We British have a great capacity for tiptoeing round a subject without saying anything at all.

PAULINE: Like you're doing now.

[WILLIAM *smiles then looks off* S/L.]

WILLIAM: Ah, the wanderers return.

[*STAN, BERNICE and a recalcitrant* MOTHER *enter* S/L.]

STAN: Running off like that! You scared the life out of us!

MOTHER: I did not run off! I haven't run for years.

STAN: Well, creep off then.

MOTHER: Oh, I'm a snake now, am I?

BERNICE: Nobody mentioned snakes, Mother. Now come and sit down.

MOTHER: And will you stop pulling me? You'll have my arm out of its socket in a minute!

          [*But she does allow herself to be sat down in her chair.*]

BERNICE: [*to* PAULINE] And where were you when this was going on?

PAULINE: I went for a walk. I told you I was going for a walk!

STAN: All right, let's all calm down now. Mother's back – crisis over. [*noticing*] Oh, no, where's Margaret?

WILLIAM: She was part of the search-party, Stan, if you remember. You sent her the other way.

STAN: Oh, yes.

WILLIAM: She was going as far as the National Trust shop and back. There's no need to worry about Margaret.

STAN: Sorry, William, it's just that it's been a very stressful start to the holiday – very stressful.

MOTHER: Calling me a snake.

STAN: Mother, nobody called you a snake!

BERNICE: I know. Why don't we all sit down and have a nice drink? Sparkling white wine anybody?

STAN: I fancy a cup of tea.

PAULINE: Me too. I'll get the Thermos.

          [PAULINE *goes into their hut to do this.*]

BERNICE: Cup of tea, Mother?

MOTHER: I'd sooner have an ice cream.

STAN: I'll get you one later.

BERNICE: Just me for the sparkling white wine then, is it?

> [*Nobody answers so she pours herself one and sits down.* PAULINE *comes out of the hut with two mugs of tea and hands one to* STAN, *who takes it gratefully.*]

STAN: Thanks, Pauline.

> [*He and* PAULINE *sit down.*]

Ah, that's better.

> [MARGARET *enters* S/R.]

MARGARET: Oh, good, we're all re-united.

WILLIAM: Hello, my dear.

STAN: Thanks for looking for Mother, Margaret.

MARGARET: Not at all.

MOTHER: I'm here.

MARGARET: Yes, I can see that.

MOTHER: Well, why are you looking for me?

STAN: Margaret *was* looking for you.

MOTHER: Well, she can stop because I'm here.

BERNICE: But you weren't then . . . Oh, never mind. A sparkling white wine, Margaret?

MARGARET: No thanks. I'll just have a sit-down and enjoy the sunshine.

> [MARGARET *sits down and peace descends on the whole group.*]

STAN: Now, this is it, isn't it? This is what beach hut life is all about. The right kind of people just relaxing together.

> [DOUG *enters* S/L, *pulling an already inflated dinghy behind him. He is in his thirties, expensively dressed in shorts and shirt and cheerfully and confidently working-class.*]

DOUG: Morning, morning! I'm looking for number . . . [*looking at the middle hut*] Cancel the looking. I've found it. [*shouting and waving his hands* S/R] Over here, girls! I've found it! Over here!

             [*His rather raucous manner makes* STAN, BERNICE, WILLIAM *and* MARGARET *flinch.* STAN *also doesn't like the fact that the dinghy, which* DOUG *has let go of, is impinging on 'his' space.* DOUG *looks at the middle hut with some disapproval.*]

             I'll tell you what, it looked better in the photograph. Bit dilapidated, isn't it?

             [*He produces a key, opens up the middle hut and looks in.*]

             Blimey, I've seen bigger garden sheds than this! Are yours as small?

BERNICE: We find ours quite sufficiently adequate, thank you.

DOUG: We were thinking of kipping down here some nights, you see.

MARGARET: Oh, you're not allowed to sleep in them.

DOUG: Who says?

STAN: One of the rules.

DOUG: Rules! They're taking over the world, rules.

STAN: We'd be in a funny old mess without them.

DOUG: Lot happier, though.

STAN: You're not an anarchist, are you?

DOUG: An anarchist? Me? No, I'm in fish.

             [*Unexpectedly, this makes* PAULINE *laugh.*]

             [*looking off*] Come on you two! Dear oh dear, you *are* out of condition.

             [DEBS *and* BECKY *enter* S/R. *They are both attractive twenty-somethings, wearing short robes over their swimsuits. They are carrying a selection of*

> *bags and are out of breath. They put their bags*
> *down carelessly – not in what* STAN *would call*
> *'their' space.*]

DEBS: You sent us the wrong way round. Show us your belly!

> [DOUG *pulls up his shirt, breathing in as he does so.*]

DOUG: There you are – flat as a pancake.

DEBS: Until you stop holding your breath.

> [DOUG *has to breathe out.*]

BECKY: Pancake! That's more like a soufflé.

> [BECKY *unfastens her robe and shows her belly –*
> *to good advantage as she is wearing a bikini. She*
> *pats her belly.*]

That's what you call flat as a pancake!

WILLIAM: You look in very good condition to me.

MARGARET: William!

BECKY: No, that's all right. Nice compliment, that is. Thank you very much.

WILLIAM: Not at all.

> [DEBS *has been looking at the middle hut.*]

DEBS: Is that it?

DOUG: That's what I said.

DEBS: It's no bigger than a garden shed.

DOUG: I said that as well.

BECKY: Well, come on, who's coming for a swim?

DEBS: Oh, yes, lovely.

BECKY: [*to* DOUG] Come on then, tubby – race you!

> [BECKY, DEBS *and* DOUG *exit* S/L, *laughing and*
> *shouting.* MOTHER *has fallen asleep but the others*
> *look on with amazement as the trio run off.*]

STAN: Well!

BERNICE: Well!

MARGARET: Well, well!

WILLIAM: [*thinking of the girls*] Well, well, well!

PAULINE: They seem a jolly lot.

STAN: Jolly? Raucous is the word I'd use! [*getting up and pacing about*] And look at this mess! Just look at it! We've had encroachment all morning and now we are being encroached upon from within!

              [*Aided by* BERNICE, *he starts to put the trio's bags and the dinghy within the confines of the middle hut's space.* DOUG *enters* S/L.]

DOUG: Only forgot the boat, didn't I? [*seeing* STAN *and* BERNICE *at work*] What's the game then?

STAN: It's not a game, my friend. We are establishing perimeters.

              [*To emphasize the point,* BERNICE *makes three imaginary rectangles with her hands.*]

BERNICE: You know – perimeters.

DOUG: Oh, got you. I thought this was all communal.

MARGARET: Communal?

DOUG: Yes. Anyway, don't worry. It will sort itself out.

              [*He starts to pull the dinghy off* S/L.]

STAN: Nothing sorts itself . . .

DOUG: See you later. If we're not back soon, we've paddled over to France for lunch.

              [DOUG *has gone so* STAN *addresses the others.*]

STAN: Nothing sorts itself out! It doesn't!

MARGARET: I hate the word 'communal'.

WILLIAM: Pretty girls, though.

MARGARET: That's beside the point.

STAN: Exactly. Pretty girls are irrelevant. Right, I'm off.

BERNICE: Where to?

STAN: To take steps, that's where to. I'm going to the village.

MOTHER: [*waking up*] What about my ice cream?

STAN: What ice cream?

MOTHER: The one I wanted just after I was called a snake.

STAN: Mother . . . Oh, look, come on. I'll walk you up to the kiosk. Pauline, do you think you could come with me and walk Mother back?

> [MOTHER *gets up.*]

MOTHER: I don't need walking back.

> [PAULINE *gets up as well.*]

PAULINE: I'll come anyway – just for the company.

> [STAN, PAULINE *and* MOTHER *start to move off.*]

BERNICE: Stan, what is it you're going to buy?

STAN: A deterrent, that's what!

> [STAN, PAULINE *and* MOTHER *exit* S/L.]

BERNICE: What does he mean – a deterrent?

WILLIAM: Perhaps he's going to buy those machine-guns I mentioned.

MARGARET: It's not a laughing matter, William. You seem to find everything a laughing matter these days.

WILLIAM: My dear old girl, these are the days for finding everything a laughing matter.

> [*Strangely, this produces a moment of tenderness between* WILLIAM *and* MARGARET. BERNICE *is curious.*]

BERNICE: Anything I should know about?

WILLIAM: No, no. Just a private joke.

BERNICE: Oh. So what about *them*? [*nodding towards the middle hut*] They're a funny trio, aren't they?

MARGARET: 'Funny' is not a word which would have sprung to the very front of my mind.

BERNICE: I was being ironical actually. And what about those girls?

WILLIAM: Yes, what *about* those girls?

BERNICE: I meant there being two of them – and only one of him.

MARGARET: He talked of them sleeping in the beach hut.

BERNICE: Exactly, Margaret. No wonder my insides turned to jelly when I heard the word 'renters'.

WILLIAM: Does it really matter? We aren't here at nights anyway.

BERNICE: No, but they would be – all three of them.

MARGARET: [*thoughtfully*] Yes.

WILLIAM: Well, perhaps they're strapped for cash. Perhaps they can't afford an hotel.

MARGARET: There are several little B & Bs in the village. Perfectly nice in their own way, I'm sure.

BERNICE: I wonder what he does.

WILLIAM: With the two girls, you mean?

BERNICE: For a living!

MARGARET: He did say he was in fish.

BERNICE: Yes, I know, but that could mean anything, couldn't it?

[*She nods towards the trio's bags. MARGARET takes the hint and joins BERNICE, who is edging towards the middle hut.*]

MARGARET: Not that one can judge anything by beach bags.

BERNICE: No, one can't. Still . . .

[*They edge closer, looking at the bags in an appraising way. DOUG enters S/L and is amused by what he sees.*]

DOUG: Looking for something?

[BERNICE *and* MARGARET *spring away from the bags.*]

BERNICE: No. no. We were just . . .

MARGARET: Just looking after your things.

DOUG: [*not believing this for a moment*] Oh. I see. That's very neighbourly of you. Oars.

MARGARET: I beg your pardon?

DOUG: Oars for the dinghy. I forgot them.

> [*He rummages around looking for the oars.* MARGARET *gestures to* WILLIAM. *He does not understand her.*]

WILLIAM: [*mouthing*] What?

> [MARGARET *gestures again and this time* WILLIAM *gets it.*]

By the way, we haven't introduced ourselves. I'm William and this is my wife. Margaret.

DOUG: Oh. how do? I'm Doug.

BERNICE: And I'm Bernice Billet. You've already met my husband. Stan. and my sister. Pauline.

DOUG: How do you do?

BERNICE: And Stan's mother. of course.

DOUG: The old girl with the brolly.

BERNICE: Elderly lady. yes.

MARGARET: And the two young ladies?

> [DOUG *realizes what they are after and decides to play them along.*]

DOUG: Oh. right. They're Debs and Becky.

MARGARET: I see.

DOUG: Deborah and Rebecca in full.

WILLIAM: Pretty girls.

DOUG: Yes. they are. aren't they?

MARGARET: And they would be?

DOUG: Well. Debs is a hairdresser and Rebecca works for a building society.

MARGARET: Ah.

BERNICE: I think Margaret was meaning more along the lines of your relationship.

DOUG: Oh, right.

> [*He says no more.*]

MARGARET: Not that it's any of our business.

DOUG: Oh, it's no secret. Me and Debs and Becky do have a relationship all right.

> [*He lets them stew for a minute.*]

They're my nieces.

> [*Nobody believes this for a moment.*]

BERNICE: Nieces?

DOUG: That's right.

MARGARET: Both of them?

DOUG: They're sisters.

WILLIAM: Good Lord.

DOUG: Anything else?

MARGARET: Pardon?

DOUG: Well, we've done the introductions. I wondered if there was anything else you wanted to know.

MARGARET: Oh, I do hope you didn't think we were prying.

DOUG: No, the thought never crossed my mind.

BERNICE: If beach hut life has taught us anything it is to respect other people's privacy.

DOUG: Quite right too.

BERNICE: You said you were in fish.

DOUG: That's right. Well, fish and chips to be exact.

BERNICE: Really?

WILLIAM: I've always considered fish and chips to be one of the rocks upon which the British Empire was built.

DOUG: I couldn't agree more.

WILLIAM: A pity they stopped serving them in newspaper. They never tasted quite the same after that.

DOUG: I'm with you there, William. Another petty rule – there's too many petty rules. I mean, you think of it. You could eat your fish and chips and digest the news at the same time.

WILLIAM: [*chuckling*] That's rather good.

DOUG: Thank you.

            [BERNICE *is not pleased to see them getting on so well.*]

            Well, if we're ever going to get this boat launched . . .

            [*But before* DOUG *can leave,* PAULINE *enters with* MOTHER S/L.]

MOTHER: It fell off.

BERNICE: What did?

PAULINE: Her ice cream, but she'd nearly finished it anyway.

MOTHER: I had not! I was just coming to the best bit but the cone got all soggy and the ice cream fell off.

DOUG: Never mind, Ma. Me and the girls will be having one later. I'll bring you back another one.

MOTHER: Who are you? I've seen you before.

BERNICE: This is Doug, Mother. He's rented the middle hut.

MOTHER: I don't like nuts.

DOUG: Right, I'll remember that. [*to* PAULINE] Have you had a swim yet?

PAULINE: No, I haven't.

            [*Is there some instant attraction?*]

DOUG: Tell you what, fancy a dip with me and the girls?

BERNICE: I don't think Pauline . . .

PAULINE: Thank you, yes I would. It's no fun swimming on your own.

DOUG: Come on then.

[DOUG *and* PAULINE *exit* S/L.]

BERNICE:	Well!
MARGARET:	Well, well!
WILLIAM:	Well, well, well!
MOTHER:	He's nicely set up, isn't he?
BERNICE:	That's not the point.
MOTHER:	I didn't say it was.
BERNICE:	I mean, how many women does he want?
WILLIAM:	They've only gone for a swim.
BERNICE:	Things have started with people only going for a swim.
MOTHER:	If God had intended us to swim he would have given us fins.
MARGARET:	William taught our boys to swim when they were very young, didn't you, William?
WILLIAM:	Yes I did. Where do the years go?
MARGARET:	Both married now, with children of their own.
BERNICE:	I bet they don't run a fish and chip shop.
MARGARET:	Well, no. Peter's a solicitor and Roger's in the Royal Navy.
BERNICE:	That's what I mean, you see. They're *proper* people.
WILLIAM:	Personally, I think Doug's rather a chummy chap.
BERNICE:	But he's not the Woodersons, is he?

[WILLIAM *looks at his watch and gets up.*]

WILLIAM:	[*to* MARGARET] Well, I think it's time we toddled off for a spot of lunch.
MARGARET:	[*getting up*] Good idea, yes.
WILLIAM:	Best get the table and chairs in, I suppose.
BERNICE:	Leave them out if you want to. We'll be here. I've done us some baguettes.
MARGARET:	That's very kind. See you later then.

[WILLIAM *and* MARGARET *exit* S/L.]

WILLIAM: [*as they go*] Do you know what I'm in the mood for? Some fish and chips.

> [BERNICE *takes her two chairs away from* WILLIAM *and* MARGARET'*s table and puts them back in 'her' space, tutting at* DOUG'*s litter of bags as she does so.*]

MOTHER: If God had intended us to swim he would have given us fins.

BERNICE: You said that.

MOTHER: Well, now I'm saying it again.

BERNICE: What about a nice nap?

MOTHER: I'll decide when I want a nap, thank you.

BERNICE: Very well, Mother.

MOTHER: I'll have one now.

BERNICE: Come on then.

> [*She goes to help.*]

MOTHER: Stop pulling me about!

BERNICE: I'm not pulling, I'm helping.

> [*She tries to usher* MOTHER *into their hut.*]

MOTHER: You're pushing now!

BERNICE: Oh, for goodness' sake!

> [*She gets* MOTHER *into the hut.* STAN *enters* S/L. *carrying four bulging plastic bags.*]

STAN: This'll show them! This'll show them!

> [*Seeing no one about he talks more loudly.*]

> I said: 'This'll show them! This'll show them!'

> [BERNICE *comes out of the hut.*]

BERNICE: Show who what?

STAN: Where's Mother? You haven't let her wander off again, have you?

BERNICE: I've put her down for a nap.

STAN: Oh. Good.

BERNICE:	Show who what?
STAN:	The encroachers, that's who!

> [*He puts his bags down and from one of them he produces a plastic pot with plastic flowers in it.*]

Look at that!

BERNICE:	[*puzzled*] I don't see that giving them flowers is going to do any good.
STAN:	Don't be absurd, Bernice. They aren't gifts. They are our perimeters.

> [BERNICE *still looks puzzled but then* STAN *takes more plastic pots and flowers from the bags and starts to use them to mark out a rectangle in front of their hut.* BERNICE *catches on.*]

BERNICE:	Oh, I see!

> [STAN *gives one of* DOUG*'s 'encroaching' bags a kick.*]

STAN:	And that can move over there for a start!

> [BERNICE *helps him with the flowerpots.*]

BERNICE:	How far down are we going?
STAN:	I thought about here would be reasonable.
BERNICE:	What if nobody takes them seriously?
STAN:	Look at it this way. Encroachers or not, nobody actually stands on your beach towel, do they?
BERNICE:	Well, no.
STAN:	So think of this area as a big beach towel. It's down and possession is nine tenths of the law.
BERNICE:	It's a bit German, isn't it?
STAN:	No it is not German! It's my idea and it's British. Anyway, it's not intended to bag a lounger by the pool, it's intended to protect what is rightfully ours.
BERNICE:	Unofficially.
STAN:	Look here, you're not starting to waver, are you?

BERNICE: I'm just thinking of what William said. It is all unofficial, isn't it?

STAN: I'm afraid William let the side down on that one. Where is William, by the way?

BERNICE: He and Margaret have gone off for some lunch.

STAN: Oh.

[*The flowerpots are in place now, arranged in their rectangle.*]

There!

[STAN *stands inside the rectangle as though it were a little fort.*]

I'll get William and Margaret some of these if they'd like them.

BERNICE: What about Doug?

STAN: He can get his own.

BERNICE: No, I mean what if he doesn't take to them?

STAN: Then tough toenails. He's got to learn to respect the rules like everybody else.

BERNICE: Unofficial rules.

STAN: Will you stop saying that? I don't know what's wrong with you, Bernice, but you're becoming a quivering jelly of doubt.

BERNICE: Well, it's not as united as when the Woodersons were here. William seems to be taking it all very lightly and with that lot in the middle . . .

STAN: Oh, don't worry about him. I've met his sort before. I'll soon have him in line. Where is he anyway?

BERNICE: He dragged Pauline down to the beach.

STAN: Dragged?

BERNICE: Well – asked.

STAN: And she agreed?

BERNICE: Obviously.

STAN: [*shaking his head*] I don't know.

BERNICE: He runs a fish and chip shop.

STAN: Does he? And what about his so-called nieces? Are they down there too?

BERNICE: Yes. I suppose you could say safety in numbers.

STAN: I don't know about that. He had two to begin with.

[BERNICE *sits down.*]

BERNICE: Sparkling white wine?

STAN: [*joining her*] Yes, I think I will.

[BERNICE *pours him a glass.* STAN *notices the bottle.*]

Have you got through that already?

BERNICE: I don't like the expression 'got through'. You know Doctor Windlass said I needed plenty of liquid.

STAN: I'm not sure he meant sparkling white wine.

BERNICE: Let me be the judge of that.

STAN: Sorry, Bernice. I just feel very on edge. This holiday seems to have got off entirely on the wrong foot.

BERNICE: I know. [*pointing to the beach*] That lot down there seem to be getting out of hand. [*pointing to the middle hut*] And that lot – well!

STAN: They just don't fit, do they? Think of the Woodersons. I mean, you could go a whole couple of days without speaking to the Woodersons. That's the sort of people we want up here.

[DOUG *and* PAULINE – *a decidedly happier* PAULINE – *enter* S/L. DOUG *is holding a piece of seaweed, which he tosses at* STAN.]

DOUG: There you go, Stan – I caught you an eel.

[STAN *flaps wildly at the seaweed.*]

STAN: Get it off! Get it off!

PAULINE: It's seaweed, Stan.

STAN: Oh, very humorous. I'm sure.

PAULINE: We had a lovely swim.

BERNICE: Did you?

PAULINE: Mucking about, you know.

BERNICE: Yes.

[DOUG *looks at the flowerpots.*]

DOUG: Blimey, they grew quickly.

STAN: They're artificial, as you can well see.

DOUG: So they are. What are they for?

STAN: Would you like to sit down please?

[*He gestures to the empty chair inside the rectangle.*]

DOUG: You mean I can come in?

STAN: Of course you can come in!

DOUG: Anywhere I like or is there a door?

STAN: Just sit down please!

[DOUG *sits down on the empty chair.*]

Now see here, Doug, there are a few beach hut rules that I think I should acquaint you with.

PAULINE: I think I'll go and get changed.

BERNICE: Don't wake Mother. You know how funny she goes if she's woken suddenly.

PAULINE: No, all right.

[*She goes into their hut.*]

DOUG: No need to close the door.

[PAULINE *smiles at* DOUG. *But she does close the door.*]

STAN: These ground rules!

DOUG: Sorry. Yes?

STAN: Well . . .

DOUG: Who made them up, by the way, you?

STAN:	No, not me personally. I suppose they just evolved over the years amongst the beach hut people.
BERNICE:	Organically, you might say.
DOUG:	I see. So you've got organic ground rules which aren't actually legal, is that right?
	[STAN *and* BERNICE *do not like the drift of this.*]
STAN:	In so many words, yes.
BERNICE:	But we all respect them. If we didn't, the whole community would go haywire.
DOUG:	[*mock serious*] Would it really?
STAN:	It would. Now, as a newcomer, we wouldn't expect you to know all the rules.
DOUG:	Well, that would be tricky as they're unwritten. Could you give me the general gist to be getting on with?
STAN:	Well, yes. A respect for each other's privacy.
BERNICE:	Like changing without shutting the door.
DOUG:	Heaven forbid.
STAN:	Keeping one's stuff within one's confines.
	[*He points to the bags outside the middle hut.*]
DOUG:	You've moved that lot, haven't you?
STAN:	Very carefully and only to within your confines.
	[BERNICE *makes her 'perimeters' gesture again.*]
DOUG:	I see. Are the flowerpots compulsory then?
STAN:	No, no. They are symbolic. They are saying to the beach people: 'Respect our space.'
DOUG:	This is legally our space then?
STAN:	Not legally in so many words.
DOUG:	Oh, another unwritten one?
STAN:	Yes.
BERNICE:	Then there's the sleeping thing.
DOUG:	There's not an unwritten law about having a nap, is there?

BERNICE: I meant sleeping at nights.

DOUG: What time do we have to be in bed by then?

BERNICE: You mentioned sleeping in the beach hut!

DOUG: Oh, that. You don't have to worry about that. I changed my mind as soon as I saw it. I thought they'd be more like chalets. Who in their right mind would want to sleep in a shed? No, me and the girls will book in somewhere.

STAN: There are some decent little B & Bs in the village.

DOUG: I don't like B & Bs. Bed and boredom, I call them.

BERNICE: I'm afraid our hotel is fully booked.

DOUG: That's all right. We'll book in at that hotel up along the cliffs.

              [STAN *and* BERNICE *react to this.*]

STAN: The Royal . . . ? That's a five-star hotel!

DOUG: Good. More stars the merrier, I say.

              [STAN *and* BERNICE *are open-mouthed as* PAULINE *comes out of the hut, now in a summer dress.*]

PAULINE: [*to* STAN *and* BERNICE] Why are your mouths open?

STAN: Well, Doug's talking about booking in at . . .

              [*He points in the direction of the hotel on the cliffs.*]

BERNICE: And without being in any way patronizing, Doug did say he was in fish and chips.

DOUG: Well, I am.

PAULINE: He's winding you up. He's got *some* fish and chip shops.

BERNICE: Some?

DOUG: Well, yes. A sort of chain, I suppose you'd call it.

STAN: A chain?

DOUG: I started with one – well, I suppose you'd have to start with one – when I took over from my old mum and dad. Got about twenty now.

[STAN *and* BERNICE *gawp again.*]

Do you know the secret?

STAN: No, what?

DOUG: Batter.

STAN: Batter?

DOUG: Batter. My old mum, she said: 'Get your batter right and you can't go far wrong.' Wise words, those. Sorry, Stan, I've got you off the subject. You were talking about unwritten ground rules.

STAN: Was I? Oh, yes.

DOUG: We'd done the sleeping arrangements, the not chang-ing without shutting the door and the flowerpots.

STAN: I do wish you wouldn't call them flowerpots.

DOUG: Well, they are.

STAN: But they represent so much more!

DOUG: Like a barricade against the riff-raff?

STAN: In so many words, yes.

DOUG: Understood. In other words, once I'm out of here, there's no way I can get back in, right?

BERNICE: Oh, no. You're not riff-raff. You own a chain of premises. You can't be riff-raff.

DOUG: Oh, I see.

STAN: Not in any way that it's a class thing. It's a behav-iour thing.

MOTHER: [*from inside the hut, singing*]
                    'These boots are made for walking,
                    And that's just what they'll do.
                    One of these days these boots
                    Are going to walk right over you.'
            [*Silence.* DOUG *looks enquiringly at the hut.*]

STAN: Don't mind Mother. She does sometimes sing in her sleep.

PAULINE: It's a behaviour thing.

[BERNICE *is about to reply but spots something off* S/R *and reacts with alarm.*]

BERNICE:	Oh, no! Stan, look!
STAN:	Oh, no, they've joined forces!
DOUG:	Who, the Sioux and the Cheyenne?
STAN:	Worse!

[MRS. PENFOLD, MRS. NEWMAN *and* IDA *march on* S/R. MRS. PENFOLD *points to* STAN *and* BERNICE.]

MRS. P:	Are they the ones?
IDA:	They're the ones!
MRS. N:	They're the ones!
MRS. P:	Right next to the other ones!
DOUG:	[*to* STAN *and* BERNICE] Have they seen your faces on a 'wanted' poster or what?
MRS. P:	Who are you?
DOUG:	I'm a reporter from *Hello!* Magazine.
MRS. N:	Well, you report this then. They think they own the world, these two.
MRS. P:	And the other two.
DOUG:	What other two?
MRS. P:	The old posh ones.
STAN:	Now see here . . .
MRS. P:	No, *you* see here. The three of us met on the beach and all our stories corrob. . . corrob. . . they all agreed.
STAN:	I've never seen you before in my life.
MRS. P:	No, but your posh friends have. All I did was come up here to look for a kite and what did I get? Being treated like rubbish, that's what I got!
IDA:	Well, you've seen me before. All I wanted was a nice sit-down and I was fobbed off with a load of codswallop about this being private property!
STAN:	I refute codswallop!

BERNICE: Stan was merely . . . merely . . .

DOUG: Waffling?

BERNICE: Well, yes, but only in everyone's best interests.

IDA: Yours, you mean. I don't like being played with and if I hadn't met Mrs. Penfold here I'd never have known I had been!

MRS. N: Two kids nearly wetting themselves and you wouldn't even let them use your toilet!

STAN: For the last time, we do not have a toilet!

MRS. N: That's not the point.

STAN: Well, what is?

MRS. P: Your high-handed attitude!

BERNICE: We are not high-handed. We simply seek to maintain the natural order of things.

MRS. P: Yes, you at the top and everybody else at the bottom. Well, you, madam, and you, Sonny Jim, have got it coming!

MRS. N: In spades!

[STAN *is frightened by this.*]

STAN: What do you mean?

MRS. P: Never you mind! Come on, girls!

[MRS. PENFOLD. MRS. NEWMAN *and* IDA *exit* S/R. PAULINE *and* DOUG *are tickled by this incident but* STAN *and* BERNICE *are shaken.*]

PAULINE: 'Hubble bubble, toil and trouble' wasn't it?

STAN: What was?

PAULINE: The three witches in *Macbeth.*

STAN: Don't make light of it, Pauline, they're insane.

PAULINE: Of course they're not insane. They're just angry. You should be nicer to people.

BERNICE: Stan's always nicer to people. He was just defending our rights.

PAULINE: We don't have any rights!

DOUG: Never mind, Stan, you've got your flowerpots.

BERNICE: Good riddance to them.

STAN: My flowerpots?

BERNICE: No, those awful women.

STAN: But it isn't good riddance. You heard what they said. 'You've got it coming,' they said. What have we got coming? What do they mean?

PAULINE: Perhaps they've put a curse on you.

BERNICE: Pauline, that is not funny!

PAULINE: Oh, they were venting their feelings, that's all. We probably won't see them again.

DOUG: Unless they're planning a night attack. Perhaps you should sleep down here, Stan.

STAN: [*taken in for a moment*] Nobody's allowed to sleep down . . . [*catching on*] Oh, very funny! Why am I the only one taking this seriously?

BERNICE: I'm taking it seriously, Stan.

STAN: Well, thank goodness for that. I mean, anything could happen – anything!

> [*He looks despairing and* BERNICE *comforts him.* DEBS *and* BECKY *enter* S/L. *They are both wearing bikinis and are trailing their robes.*]

DEBS: The water's lovely and warm.

BECKY: And we met some ever so nice Italians.

DOUG: You should have asked them to lunch.

BECKY: We didn't like to straight off.

DOUG: Why not? The more the merrier.

> [BERNICE *is shocked by her own interpretation of this.*]

How about you, Pauline – are you on for lunch?

BERNICE: I don't think Pauline . . .

PAULINE:	I'd love to. Thanks.
DOUG:	I'll get on the mobile in a minute. Book a table up at the hotel.
	[DEBS *and* BECKY *get out their beach towels and settle down on them.*]
DEBS:	Can we just have a sunbathe first?
DOUG:	Course you can. No rush. [*to* STAN *and* BERNICE] What about you two? How about joining us for a spot of lunch? It's on me.
BERNICE:	I don't think so, thank you all the same. I've done us baguettes.
STAN:	Not that I could look a baguette in the face at the moment.
BECKY:	Oh dear, you're not ill, are you?
STAN:	No, I'm sick.
BECKY:	Isn't that the same thing?
STAN:	Fed up then.
DEBS:	Who could be fed up on a lovely day like this?
STAN:	I could! You come down here for a bit of peace and quiet only to find that the world has gone mad!
DEBS:	How mad?
STAN:	I don't want to talk about it. Just mad, that's all – just mad!
	[DEBS *and* BECKY *look at each other and shrug.*]
DEBS:	Well, let's have a sunbathe.
	[*Facing* STAN, DEBS *and* BECKY *both reach for the clips of their bikini tops.*]
BECKY:	Nobody minds topless, do they?
	[STAN*'s jaw drops.*]
STAN:	Oh, my God!

END OF ACT ONE

ACT TWO

Scene 1

Early next morning.

A windbreak has now been set up just a couple of feet in front of the huts. It's quite a long windbreak too and some of STAN*'s flowerpots have been tossed aside to make room for it. Within the confines of the windbreak* MRS. PENFOLD, MRS. NEWMAN *and* IDA *sit on three canvas chairs. They are fully dressed against the morning chill.*

IDA:	What if they don't come down today?
MRS. P:	Then we'll come back tomorrow.
MRS. N:	Quite right. They've got to be shown.
IDA:	What if they don't come down tomorrow?
MRS. P:	Oh, will you stop it with your 'what ifs'? You don't win a strike with a lot of 'what ifs'.
IDA:	It's not exactly a strike, is it?
MRS. P:	All right, a protest then. Nobody has a right to what they don't have a right to and we're here to prove it.
IDA:	It's not much of a holiday for the kids, is it?
MRS. N:	They're all right. My Basil and her Ted are looking after them.
MRS. P:	In any case, we're not intending to sit up here all holiday – just long enough to prove our point. Now are we solid or not?
MRS. N:	I'm solid.
IDA:	Oh, I'm solid too.
MRS. P:	Good!

[*They all fold their arms at the same time as if to emphasize their implacability.* STAN *and* BERNICE *enter* S/L. *They are not yet wearing their beach clothes.* BERNICE *is in trousers and a blouse.*]

STAN: Mother will be all right on that coach trip, won't she?

BERNICE: Of course she will. The old people always have guards, don't they?

STAN: Guards?

BERNICE: Well, helpers then.

STAN: Nevertheless, I hope . . . I . . . I . . .

[*He trails off as he and* BERNICE *see the windbreak and the women sheltering within it. They look at each other then at the windbreak again.* MRS. PENFOLD, MRS. NEWMAN *and* IDA *stare resolutely ahead. Quite unnecessarily,* STAN *points at the windbreak.* BERNICE *indicates that he should do something about it.*]

Excuse me.

[*No response.*]

I said: 'Excuse me'.

MRS. P: Yes?

STAN: Would you mind moving that thing?

MRS. P: We're not moving, are we, girls?

MRS. N/IDA: [*together*] No.

[*Nonplussed,* STAN *looks to* BERNICE *to do something.*]

BERNICE: My husband did say 'please'.

MRS. P: He can go on his knees and beg so far as we're concerned.

BERNICE: But you're right in front of the beach huts. If we sit down we won't even be able to see the sea.

MRS. P: You'll have to stand then.

BERNICE: All right, how would you like it if I stood right in front of you?

> [*She does stand right in front of them. They are not bothered.*]

MRS. P: Stand where you like. It's a free country.

MRS. N: I don't particularly like looking at the sea anyway.

IDA: I tell you what. Those trousers do you no favours at all.

> [*This makes* BERNICE *retreat back to* STAN. *She motions to him to do something.* STAN *goes over to the three ladies.*]

STAN: I've noticed what you've done to my flowerpots.

MRS. P: Your fence, you mean, because that's what they were supposed to be – a fence around private property.

STAN: Exactly.

MRS. P: Except that it's not private property at all. None of it is.

IDA: Unlike what was intimated to me.

STAN: All right! Strictly speaking this area is not private property.

MRS. P/MRS. N/IDA: [*together*] Ah-hah!

STAN: But . . . *but* . . .

MRS. N: He hasn't got a leg to stand on.

STAN: I don't need a leg to stand on. I'm talking about common decency.

IDA: Like lying to people?

MRS. P: Like thinking that owning a beach hut makes you Lord of the Manor?

MRS. N: Like banning two little kids who are bursting?

BERNICE: All right then. Can't we appeal to your better nature?

MRS. P: So far as you're concerned we don't have a better nature.

STAN: So be it, so be it. You leave me no alternative. I am
             issuing you with a final warning!

             [*He adopts a triumphant pose. The three ladies
             are unmoved.*]

             Did you hear what I said?

MRS. P: Yes, you've issued your final warning.

STAN: And?

MRS. P: We're ignoring it.

             [STAN *raises a stern finger but then can't think
             of anything to say so he rejoins* BERNICE.]

             An empty vessel, that's what he is.

STAN: Well, let me tell you something. Let me tell you what
             we think of this charade. We couldn't care less!

MRS. N: You haven't been acting like it.

STAN: That was before we realized what utter fools you've
             been making of yourselves.

BERNICE: Yes, you don't seem to realize how ridiculous you look.
             Chairs, Stan.

STAN: Absolutely.

             [*He unlocks their hut and he and* BERNICE *get their
             chairs out and set them down in the small space
             behind the windbreak. They sit down. Only the
             tops of their heads show above the windbreak.*]

BERNICE: Well, this is very nice.

STAN: Yes it is. It is very nice.

IDA: You two look like Punch and Judy.

BERNICE: Ignore them, Stan.

STAN: I am, Bernice – completely.

MRS. P: Ooh, look what's going on down the beach!

MRS. N: Well I never!

             [*Curiosity gets the better of* STAN *and* BERNICE
             and they stand up to look over the windbreak. They

[*realize they have been had when the three ladies laugh so they sit down again.*]

BERNICE: It's amazing how childish people can be, isn't it, Stan?

STAN: It never ceases to amaze me, Bernice.

[*The three ladies are amused again.*]

Not that it really bothers me.

BERNICE: Oh, it doesn't bother me either. Not one jot.

STAN: Or tittle.

[*This pathetic ruse only amuses the interlopers, who whisper to each other.*]

MRS. P: Oh, well.

[*The three ladies stand up as if to go. STAN and BERNICE are immediately on their feet, ready to retake 'their' space, but the ladies sit down again, making the couple look sillier than ever.*]

STAN: Look, are you going to move or not?

MRS. P/MRS. N/IDA: [*together*] No!

[STAN *looks close to despair but brightens up as he looks off* S/R.]

STAN: William! William and Margaret!

[WILLIAM *and* MARGARET *enter* S/R.]

WILLIAM: Good morning. I was just . . .

[*He and* MARGARET *stop as they see the windbreak and the three ladies sitting there.*]

Oh dear.

MARGARET: Might one ask what is going on?

MRS. P: [*mimicking*] Oh, by all means one might.

MRS. N: We're demonstrating.

MARGARET: Stupidity presumably?

MRS. P: Here we go – hardly sooner arrived than the upper-class insults start flying.

WILLIAM: You must admit this is all very petty.

IDA: Not to us it's not. It's a matter of principle. Despite the illusion that we were given, this is not private property and we are here to prove it.

MRS. N/IDA: [*together*] Yes!

MARGARET: Knowing full well that you are blocking our view?

MRS. P/MRS. N/IDA: [*together*] Yes.

WILLIAM: I think this is called an impasse.

MRS. P: That's it – use words we don't understand.

WILLIAM: A stalemate then.

STAN: I did give them a final warning.

MARGARET: Then why are they still here?

STAN: They ignored it.

> [*To the further amusement of the three ladies, STAN and BERNICE join WILLIAM and MARGARET for a little conference.*]

MARGARET: Well, what's to be done?

BERNICE: I was rather hoping that William could pull a rabbit out of the hat.

WILLIAM: What sort of rabbit?

BERNICE: A legal one. You did say you were in the profession.

WILLIAM: Well, yes, but I specialized in copyright law.

BERNICE: There's no chance you could copyright sand?

WILLIAM: None.

STAN: Isn't there some other stroke you could pull?

WILLIAM: Stroke?

STAN: Gambit then.

WILLIAM: I'm afraid not. These ladies are doing nothing illegal. Let's face it, we are firing blank ammunition.

> [*The three ladies give a little cheer.*]

STAN: I hate this! I hate this!

> [*The three ladies give another little cheer.*]

	Just don't get too triumphant. We can sit you out, you know. [*to* WILLIAM *and* MARGARET] Would you like a hand out with your chairs?
WILLIAM:	To tell you the truth, I'm not over-keen on sitting be-hind that thing.
STAN:	William, please! We've got to stick together in the face of this adversity.
MARGARET:	Stan's right, William. Remember the motto of the SAS.
WILLIAM:	[*smiling*] 'Who Dashes Wins'?
BERNICE:	Isn't that 'Dares'?
WILLIAM:	So it is.
MARGARET:	So come on, William. We didn't cave in to the Gas Board so we certainly shouldn't cave in to these people.
WILLIAM:	Oh, very well.
STAN:	We'll give you a hand.

    [WILLIAM *unlocks his hut and* STAN *and* BERNICE *help him to get two chairs out and set them up behind the windbreak.*]

| MARGARET: | [*to the three ladies*] You see? This petulant display is having no effect whatsoever. |

    [*The beach-hutters all sit down, their heads sticking up over the top of the windbreak. The three ladies love this.*]

MRS. P:	No effect whatsoever?
MARGARET:	None.
MRS. P:	Not from where we're sitting.

    [STAN's *chair is the furthest out of the four. He edges it out a little more so that, by craning his neck, he is just able to see past* IDA, *who is directly in front of him. Taking his cue at the other end,* WILLIAM *does the same to see past* MRS. NEWMAN, *who is directly in front of him. There is a whis-*

> *pered conversation between the three ladies, then they spread their chairs out as far as possible, making their 'screen' more effective.* WILLIAM *can't help but see the funny side of this.*]

WILLIAM: This is rather like sitting in the cinema behind some very large people, isn't it?

STAN: [*snappily*] It's nothing like sitting in the cinema. [*instantly repentant*] I'm sorry. William. I'm sorry.

MRS. P: He's cracking up.

STAN: I am not cracking up! You'll know when I'm cracking up when they carry me off in a straitjacket!

MRS. P: We'll look forward to that.

STAN: Then keep looking, madam, keep looking!

> [*But his bravado is in vain and he and the others behind the windbreak know it. Silence falls. The* BEACHCOMBER *enters* S/R. *He is carrying his metal detector but not 'sweeping' with it. He surveys the group.*]

BEACHCOMBER: Now that's what I like to see – people getting together.

> [*They all simply stare at him.*]

You know what they say, don't you? If four British people get on an empty bus they each sit in a different corner. It's not true. This little island of ours has made us all neighbours. Age – class – none of it matters. We can chum up with the best of them!

> [*They all keep on staring.*]

If anyone's got a camera I could take a group photograph of you. Would you like that?

> [*Mutters in the negative from everyone.*]

No? All right. Sorry to interrupt a lovely day. You just go on enjoying yourselves. Cheerio!

> [*He exits* S/R. *Is there a moment of guilt about this silly stand-off?*]

STAN: I'd like to say something.

> [*Everyone looks at him.*]

I don't know that man from Adam but there was something in what he said, wasn't there?

> [*Muttered reluctant agreement.*]

Now there have been some silly things said this morning – some hasty things. [*to the three ladies*] But we're quite prepared to overlook them if you'll just move the windbreak.

> [BERNICE, WILLIAM *and* MARGARET *wince at this gaffe.* IDA *produces a Thermos flask.*]

IDA: What about a nice cup of tea, girls?

> [*Everyone knows that they are back where they started.*]

MRS. P: We had only intended to stay for an hour – just to make our point.

MRS. N: But that was before.

IDA: Right!

MRS. P: Right!

> [DOUG *enters cheerfully* S/L.]

DOUG: Morning all! The girls will be . . .

> [*He stops as he sees the tableau then laughs.*]

STAN: It's not funny!

DOUG: It is from where I'm standing. [*to the beach-hutters*] You look as though you're sitting in the back row of a badly designed cinema.

WILLIAM: That's what I said.

DOUG: Mind you, the old back row had its advantages.

WILLIAM: Oh, it did indeed. I remember when Margaret and I were courting, we . . .

MARGARET: William!

WILLIAM: Oh, yes. Sorry.

DOUG:	Some other time, William. [*to the three ladies*] So what's going on?
MRS. P:	Ask them.
DOUG:	All right. [*to the beach-hutters*] So what *is* going on?
STAN:	As you can see for yourself, we are having trouble with windbreakers.
DOUG:	Windbreakers?
STAN:	Yes.
DOUG:	Well, I don't see that as a crisis.
BERNICE:	[*hopefully*] Don't you?
DOUG:	No. I mean, we are in the open air and if someone is having a digestive problem . . .
STAN:	You're just being crude! You know very well what I mean!
DOUG:	Sorry, Stan. Is it all right if I talk to the other side?
STAN:	There *is* no talking to them.
DOUG:	Well, I'll have a go anyway.

> [*He goes over to the three ladies.*]

	Ladies – *why?*
MRS. P:	You're that reporter from *Hello!*, aren't you?
DOUG:	'What? Oh, that. I was just having a little joke.
MRS. P:	I see. Somebody else having a joke at our expense. Well, the joke's on the other foot now.
DOUG:	Oh, it is just a joke then?
MRS. P:	No it is not! We are here to prove that all this stuff about perimeters and private property is so much tosh!
IDA:	So you can put that in your pipe and smoke it!
MRS. N:	Because we are not moving!

> [DOUG *goes back to the beach-hutters.*]

DOUG:	Well, that's that sorted out.
STAN:	You haven't sorted anything out!

DOUG: No, put like that, I suppose I haven't.

            [*He moves towards his hut.*]

STAN: Where are you going?

DOUG: Getting changed. I'm going for a swim.

STAN: You can't go for a swim at a time like this!

DOUG: Well, there's not much else to do, is there?

            [*He unlocks his hut and goes in, leaving the door open. He then re-appears.*]

            Whoops! Sorry!

            [*He pulls the door shut.*]

STAN: Did you see that? Did you see that? It's typical of a renter, isn't it? He might own a chain of fish and chip shops but where is he when the chips are down?

WILLIAM: That was rather good – 'when the chips are down'!

            [STAN *looks frustrated.* BERNICE *goes up to* MARGARET *and whispers to her.* MARGARET *nods agreement then goes over to the three ladies.*]

MARGARET: What if I were to write you a cheque?

MRS. P: A bribe, you mean?

MARGARET: I prefer to call it an inducement.

            [*The three ladies whisper amongst themselves. Is a settlement in the offing?*]

MRS. P: How much of an inducement did you have in mind?

MARGARET: How much did *you* have in mind?

MRS. P: Five thousand pounds.

MARGARET: You've taken leave of your senses!

BERNICE: Twenty quid in cash.

MRS. P: Five thousand pounds.

BERNICE: Fifty pounds in cash.

MRS. P: Five thousand pounds.

MARGARET: You've taken leave of your senses!

MRS. N: You've just said that.

STAN: Well, I'll say it as well. You've taken leave of your senses!

MRS. N: [*to* WILLIAM] Are you going to make up the three?

WILLIAM: No, madam, I am not. Your claim is plainly fatuous. You and your friends are not so much negotiating as expressing distaste for being offered any money at all. Am I right?

MRS. P: And do you blame us? Do you know how insulting it is to have money thrown at you?

WILLIAM: I've never been in a position to make a judgement.

MRS. P: Well, it is.

IDA: I think we should consider the fifty quid.

MRS. N: No we shouldn't.

IDA: What about a hundred then?

BERNICE: I am not paying you a hundred pounds.

WILLIAM: No one is paying anybody anything. Good God alive, what are we doing? It's a beautiful day, we're all on holiday and here we are wrangling about paying to sit on a strip of sand which nobody owns in the first place. There is nothing to this absurd situation which can't be solved by a simple apology.

STAN: [*to the three ladies*] So make it and we'll call it quits.

             [WILLIAM *puts his hand to his head and sits down.*]

WILLIAM: Oh, Stan!

STAN: What? What?

MRS. P: We'll have some lunch here later.

IDA: Good idea.

MRS. N: A long lunch.

             [*The unhappy status quo is restored.* DEBS *and* BECKY *enter* S/L.]

DEBS:	We've got the wrong place.
BECKY:	No we haven't. There's William. Hello, William.
DEBS:	Hello, William.
WILLIAM:	Hello, you pretty young things. Come to join the circus?
DEBS:	Sorry?
STAN:	[*standing and indicating*] This! This!
	[DEBS *and* BECKY *take in the scene.*]
BECKY:	Why are you all jammed together like that?
	[*Everybody looks to somebody else to explain.*]
DEBS:	Are we missing out on a joke or what?
STAN:	This is not a joke – it's a farce!
	[PAULINE *enters* S/L. *She stops when she sees the tableau.*]
PAULINE:	What on earth is going on?
BECKY:	That's what we want to know.
	[DOUG, *ready for a swim, comes out of the hut.*]
DOUG:	Has anybody seen the band?
ALL:	Band?
DOUG:	Yes. I'm expecting the Grenadier Guards to be joining us later.
	[*Silence.*]
	Oh, come on, lighten up, do. This has got a funny side to it. Hasn't it?
PAULINE:	Could somebody please explain how this came about in the first place?
	[*Everyone except* DOUG, DEBS *and* BECKY *starts on an explanation until* DOUG *shouts above the babble.*]
DOUG:	Nudists!
	[*The noise stops as everyone looks around.*]

Thank you. [*to* PAULINE] This is the situation as I see it. [*pointing to* STAN, BERNICE, WILLIAM *and* MARGARET] Group A lay an entirely fictitious claim to this bit of sand. [*pointing to the three ladies*] Group B dispute the claim. Group A get narky. Group B get narky back and lay *their* fictitious claim to this bit of sand by parking their backsides on it. Result? Well, you can see for yourself really.

PAULINE: I've never heard anything so stupid in all my life. All it takes is for one side to move.

STAN: What are we supposed to do – carry the beach huts somewhere else?

PAULINE: [*to the three ladies*] Couldn't you move then?

MRS. P/MRS. N/IDA: [*together*] No!

PAULINE: So here we are – what? – ten adults and not one of us can find a solution. Can't *you* do something, Doug?

[*This pricks* DOUG's *vanity. He thinks for a moment.*]

DOUG: All right.

[*He sits himself down on the sand beside the three ladies inside the windbreak.*]

MRS. P: What do you think you're doing?

DOUG: Just having a sit-down.

MRS. P: Well, you can't sit there.

DOUG: Why not? It's a public beach.

MRS. P: But this bit is marked out by a private windbreak.

MRS. N: I can vouch for that because I own it – privately.

DOUG: Oh, I agree the windbreak is private property.

IDA: You got him, girls!

DOUG: But that's – what do you reckon? – poles about 2x2 – canvas about one eighth of an inch thick – not really a *lot* of private property, is it?

[*The light begins to dawn on the beach-hutters.*]

So unless I actually sit on one of your poles – which is highly unlikely – I'm not on private property at all.

> [MARGARET *is the first to catch on entirely. She picks up her chair, puts it down within the confines of the windbreak and sits down.*]

MARGARET: As you said yourself: 'It's not private property at all. None of it is.'

MRS. P: Just a minute! What if I said this windbreak constitutes a building?

> [WILLIAM *picks up his chair, puts it down beside* MARGARET *and sits down.*]

WILLIAM: Then you, madam, would be whistling in the wind.

STAN: Bernice, I've just seen a bit of beach I particularly want to sit on!

BERNICE: Would you believe it? So have I!

> [STAN *and* BERNICE *pick up their chairs and squeeze into the windbreak space.*]

DOUG: Come and sit down, Pauline. It's cosy in here.

PAULINE: That's a word I like – cosy.

> [*She snuggles up to* DOUG.]

DEBS: Well, let *us* in then!

BECKY: It's fun, this – like playing 'Sardines'.

> [DEBS *and* BECKY *now squeeze themselves into what has become a very crowded area. After a little edging up and moving of chairs, everybody fits into the confines of the windbreak – just. This makes an uncomfortable but, to the beach-hutters, a triumphant tableau.* MOTHER *enters* S/L *and looks in amazement at what she sees.*]

MOTHER: And I thought that lot on the coach outing were loonies!

END OF SCENE 1

Scene 2

The next morning.

The windbreak has gone. The door to STAN *and* BERNICE*'s beach hut is open. The other two huts are closed.* MOTHER *sits in her chair, reading a newspaper.* STAN *is happily re-arranging his plastic flowerpots, singing 'Oh What a Beautiful Morning'.* MOTHER *puts her paper down.*

MOTHER: [*disparagingly*] Viva España!

STAN: No, Mother – 'Oh What a Beautiful Morning'.

MOTHER: Yesterday I mean – on that coach trip, We'd no sooner pulled out of the hotel than they all started to sing 'Viva España'. Silly fools!

STAN: I expect they were just trying to get into the swing of things.

MOTHER: We weren't going to Spain though, were we?

STAN: No, I take your point. Where did you go?

MOTHER: It was a Mystery Tour.

STAN: That sounds exciting.

MOTHER: Exciting? We went to Bournemouth. What's more, we *knew* we were going to Bournemouth.

STAN: But you said it was a Mystery Tour.

MOTHER: Some mystery when the bus had 'Bournemouth' on the front of it.

STAN: A bit of a giveaway, I must admit.

MOTHER: This government has got a lot to answer for.

> [STAN *tries to make some sense out of this but fails, as* MARGARET *enters* S/R.]

MARGARET: Good morning.

MOTHER: Morning.

STAN: A very good morning to you, Margaret! No William?

MARGARET: He'll be along shortly. He's having a little sit in the car.

STAN: Why's that?

MARGARET: [*a little sharply*] He just fancied a little sit in the car!

STAN: Oh, right. Fair enough.

[MARGARET *unlocks the door of her hut.*]

Here, let me give you a hand.

MARGARET: Thank you.

[STAN *helps* MARGARET *to set up the two chairs and the table.*]

STAN: Quite a day yesterday, wasn't it? Quite a day!

MARGARET: I was beginning to think we'd never get rid of those women.

STAN: Oh, we got rid of them all right. Tails between their legs! Tails between their legs! The rule of law prevailed.

MARGARET: Hardly the rule of law.

STAN: Well, no, but that's all they understand, people like that. They wouldn't last five minutes in Worcester Park.

MARGARET: Is that where you live?

STAN: At the moment, yes. Reigate is our ultimate Utopia. Yes, once I really decided that we'd had enough . . .

MARGARET: Actually, it was Doug's idea.

STAN: Oh. Yes, well, strictly speaking, I suppose it was.

MARGARET: Very effective too. Not dignified but very effective.

STAN: Tails between their legs! You know, Margaret, between you and I – and excluding morality – I'm coming round to Doug. At first I thought he was a bit of a loose cannon but yesterday I have to say that he acted like a proper beach-hutter. For the right reasons too.

[MARGARET *has a little smile to herself.*]

MARGARET: And what do you think they were?

STAN: It's obvious. The realization that we beach-hutters always act in the best interests of our little community.

MARGARET: Oh, I see.

STAN: Well, that was it surely?

MARGARET: Oh, yes, I'm sure it was.

[STAN *misses any irony from* MARGARET *and nods. With her furniture set up he sets about getting out a chair from his own hut.*]

Did you enjoy your coach trip yesterday, Mrs. Billet?

MOTHER: I hated every minute of it.

MARGARET: Oh.

[BERNICE *enters* S/L.]

BERNICE: Good morning, Margaret.

MARGARET: Good morning.

BERNICE: No William?

MARGARET: He's having a little sit in the car.

BERNICE: Why would he do that?

MARGARET: [*again snappily*] He's sitting in the car, not flying to the moon!

BERNICE: Yes, of course.

[STAN *comes out of the hut with a second chair.*]

STAN: Tails between their legs, Bernice! Tails between their legs!

BERNICE: Stan, you've been saying that since yesterday.

STAN: Have I?

BERNICE: You even sat up in the night and shouted it.

STAN: I don't remember that.

BERNICE: You were asleep!

STAN: Oh. Still, it was a great moment, wasn't it – the way we put those windbreakers to flight?

BERNICE: Thank goodness Doug thought of something.

STAN: [*shortly*] Yes.

MARGARET: [*pointedly*] Stan was saying how nice it was to see Doug acting in the best interests of our little community.

BERNICE: Was he?

STAN: Well, it *was* nice, wasn't it?

MARGARET: Oh, yes.

STAN: Call me dim, but am I missing something here?

MARGARET: I think I'll go and see what William's up to.

[*She exits* S/R.]

STAN: I hate it when women do that.

BERNICE: What, go and look for their husbands?

STAN: Before she went! The way you two smirked at each other – funny looks. I fail to see that I said anything funny.

BERNICE: You didn't. You said something stupid.

STAN: I beg your pardon?

BERNICE: Doug acting in the best interests of our little community!

STAN: Well, he did.

BERNICE: Really? What was he about to do before Pauline turned up? He was going to have a swim!

STAN: Yes, but then a sense of duty got the better of him.

BERNICE: Rubbish! Lust got the better of him.

STAN: Lust?

BERNICE: Yes. Pauline said . . . [*in a little girlie voice*] 'Can't you do something, Doug?' Two minutes later the problem was solved, but not because he was acting in the best interests of our little community!

STAN: Pauline doesn't talk like that.

BERNICE: Oh, don't split hairs! He's after her and, what's more, she's falling for it.

STAN: Are you sure?

BERNICE: Oh, use your head, Stan, do. Haven't you noticed how she's perked up since we arrived?

STAN: I thought that was us.

BERNICE: It's him! You mark my words, the next thing she'll be doing is wearing that bikini she thought was too skimpy.

STAN: Oh, my God.

BERNICE: It's not *that* skimpy.

STAN: No, the full horror of it has just come rushing in on me. He's already got those two so-called nieces!

BERNICE: Well, somebody has got to have a serious word with her.

STAN: Absolutely right. When will you do it?

BERNICE: I meant you.

STAN: Me? Oh, no. I can sell 4x4s as well, if not better, than the next man, but women's goings-on are a total mystery to me.

BERNICE: [*without thinking*] Yes. [*quickly*] I mean, yes, I'll have a word with her.

STAN: What was she doing when you left the hotel?

BERNICE: Having a lie-in, I suppose. She didn't come down for breakfast.

STAN: We didn't see her for dinner last night either.

          [STAN *and* BERNICE *look at each other, both having the same awful thought.*]

BERNICE: Oh, Stan! This could be Rex Elphinstone all over again!

STAN: Yes. I didn't have much time for the man, but at least he didn't turn up with a ready-made harem!

[*They sit dejectedly in their chairs.* MARGARET *enters* S/R, *followed by* WILLIAM, *who is being helped cheerfully along by* DEBS *and* BECKY.]

MARGARET: Are you really sure you need *that* much assistance, William?

WILLIAM: Strictly speaking no, but it's a very pleasant experience.

DEBS: Anyway, we like helping him. He's sweet.

BECKY: We should call you *Uncle* William really.

[STAN *and* BERNICE *react to the word 'Uncle'.*]

MARGARET: Are you all right?

BERNICE: Yes, we're . . . we're . . .

STAN: Fine. We're fine.

MARGARET: Oh, good. Anyone for a cup of tea?

WILLIAM: I think I'd better – bring the old temperature down a bit.

[DEBS *and* BECKY *giggle.*]

MARGARET: What about you girls?

DEBS: No, thanks all the same. We're going to play volleyball with those Italians.

WILLIAM: I could come and watch.

MARGARET: I think you'd better sit down.

WILLIAM: Probably a safer idea.

[*He sits down in his chair.*]

MARGARET: [*to* STAN *and* BERNICE] Would either of you like a cup of tea?

STAN: No thanks all the same.

MARGARET: What about you, Mrs Billet?

MOTHER: What about me?

MARGARET: Would you like a cup of tea?

MOTHER: No thank you. I've got a bottle of milk stout in my handbag.

MARGARET: Tea for two then.

[*She goes into her hut.*]

DEBS: Come on then, Becky, we'd better get going.

BECKY: See you later, William!

[DEBS *and* BECKY *start to leave* S/L, *passing* STAN *and* BERNICE.]

BERNICE: Um . . .

[DEBS *and* BECKY *stop.*]

DEBS: Did you want something?

BERNICE: Yes. Stan wanted to tell you a funny story.

[*This is news to* STAN.]

DEBS: Oh. It won't take long, will it?

BERNICE: Oh, no. You know the one, Stan – about your Uncle James.

STAN: Uncle James?

BERNICE: When you were a child in Raynes Park.

STAN: I was never a child in Raynes Park. I was a child in Motspur Park.

BERNICE: Motspur Park then! You told me about your Uncle James!

STAN: Did I?

BERNICE: Yes!

[DEBS *and* BECKY *are getting restless.*]

BECKY: Only those Italians are waiting, you see.

BERNICE: I'll tell it then. Stan's Uncle James wasn't actually related to the Billet family at all, you see – no blood – but everyone always called him *Uncle* James.

STAN: Oh, I remember now. Of course! Although he wasn't my uncle at all, I always called him Uncle.

[DEBS *and* BECKY *exchange a look. They are not stupid and know full well what* STAN *and* BERNICE *are driving at. But they are not going to cooperate.*]

DEBS: I don't want to be rude, but it's not really funny, is it, that story?

BECKY: Or did we miss something?

BERNICE: No, it's not perhaps so much a funny story as an interesting one.

DEBS: Oh, I see, yes. Well, thanks for telling us.

          [DEBS *and* BECKY *start to leave again.*]

STAN: Yes, it's strange, isn't it? The things people sometimes call each other.

BECKY: Amazing.

BERNICE: Take you two . . .

DEBS: Oh, we call each other all sorts of things, don't we, Becky?

BECKY: Yes. Then sometimes we call other people all sorts of things too. See you later!

DEBS: Ciao!

          [*She and* BECKY *exit* S/L.]

BERNICE: Well, that got us nowhere.

STAN: You should have warned me. You shouldn't have pitched me in head-first like that!

MOTHER: I remember Uncle James. He had a glass eye.

BERNICE: Thank you, Mother.

MOTHER: I think it was the left one.

          [DOUG *and* PAULINE *enter* S/R.]

PAULINE: Morning everybody.

DOUG: Morning all!

WILLIAM: Morning.

BERNICE: [*with an edge*] Good morning.

STAN: [*ditto*] Good morning.

DOUG: Glad to see you've got your flowerpots back, Stan.

STAN: Yes.

DOUG: [*to* PAULINE] So what do you want to do? Swim – go for a walk – what?

PAULINE: Oh, I'll just have a lounge about, I think. I'm a bit tired this morning.

DOUG: Good idea.

> [*He unlocks his hut and goes inside to get two chairs.* PAULINE *smiles at* STAN *and* BERNICE *but only gets frosty looks so she turns to* WILLIAM.]

PAULINE: So how are you today, William?

WILLIAM: Thinking about volleyball.

> [MARGARET *comes out of the hut with the tea-things.*]

MARGARET: The girls have gone off to play volleyball.

PAULINE: Oh, those sort of thoughts.

WILLIAM: Guilty as charged.

PAULINE: I don't know where they get the energy from, those two. They're inexhaustible.

> [STAN *and* BERNICE *gawp at what they read into this.* DOUG *comes out of his hut and sets the chairs up.*]

DOUG: Here we go.

> [*He and* PAULINE *sit down.*]

Now that's nice, isn't it? Peace, perfect peace.

> [*He and* PAULINE *look contentedly at each other.* WILLIAM *and* MARGARET *are happily pouring tea.* STAN *and* BERNICE *are a mass of tension.*]

BERNICE: We didn't see you for breakfast this morning, Pauline.

PAULINE: No you didn't.

STAN: Having a lie-in, were you?

PAULINE: You could say that.

BERNICE: You got to bed late then?

PAULINE: Not really, no.

STAN: I'm reminded of a very funny story. When I was a boy in Motspur Park we knew a chap we called Uncle James.

BERNICE: Oh, Stan, just come to the point!

STAN: All right.

> [*He stands up and faces* DOUG *and* PAULINE.]

Well?

DOUG: Well what?

STAN: Let me put it this way. This is, after all, the twenty-first century, and . . .

> [DOUG *stands up.*]

DOUG: Oh, Stan, don't keep going all round the houses. Pauline had dinner with me last night at my hotel. We spent a lovely evening together and, as fate would have it, we then spent a lovely night together. Now me and Pauline feel good about that and I'd like to think that everybody else feels good about it as well.

> [WILLIAM *and* MARGARET *are broad-minded enough to nod approval but* STAN *almost collapses into* BERNICE'S *arms as she jumps up to catch him.*]

END OF SCENE 2

Scene 3

The end of the season.

The bright sunshine has gone. Two chairs are set up outside WILLIAM *and* MARGARET*'s hut.* STAN *and* BERNICE, *dressed for departure, are bringing all their assorted baggage out of their hut and stacking it.*

STAN: Why do we always seem to go home with more stuff than we came with?

BERNICE: Your flowerpots take up four bags.

STAN: A good buy, those, though. I shall bring them again next year. I tell you what we're not bringing next year, and that's Pauline.

BERNICE: I don't know what came over her.

STAN: It's obvious – Doug.

BERNICE: Don't be crude, Stan.

STAN: I'm not being crude. I'm stating a fact. I mean, what does she see in him?

BERNICE: Well, he's quite good-looking, he's rich – charming in his own way – quite likeable really.

STAN: They're just superficial things. And what are you doing, sticking up for him all of a sudden?

BERNICE: I'm not, but to be honest, if it had just been a little holiday romance . . . well, I have been telling Pauline to come out of herself.

STAN: But not with someone who's already got two young girls in tow!

BERNICE: I know.

STAN: In tow!

BERNICE: I suppose there's no chance that they really are his nieces?

STAN: What do you think?

BERNICE: Well, we never did really find out.

STAN: We've tried. A dozen different ways we've broached the subject and all we got was evasive answers and sniggers.

BERNICE: We've never just asked the direct question, though.

STAN: How could we? What do you say? 'Excuse me, Doug, but are Debs and Becky really your nieces or are they . . . are they . . . well, your concubines?'

BERNICE: Concubines? Nobody says 'concubines' any more.

STAN: Well, what do they say?

BERNICE: Um . . . No, you're right. We can't ask a question like that.

STAN: We just have to face the unpalatable truth. Your sister has been a part of a *ménage à trois*.

BERNICE: *Ménage à quatre* – there's four of them.

[*They lapse into silence.* MOTHER *enters* S/L.]

MOTHER: I thought we were going home today.

STAN: Mother, I thought I told you to wait in the Range Rover.

MOTHER: I'm not a dog.

STAN: I didn't say you were. I'm just trying to organize things here.

MOTHER: Going round calling people dogs.

STAN: I did not . . . Oh! And where's Pauline?

MOTHER: Packing. She missed breakfast again this morning, you know. I don't think she's eating properly.

[STAN *and* BERNICE *decide to ignore this.*]

STAN: Right, well, let's go and get this show on the road. Bernice, you get Mother and some of the baggage up

                    to the car and then come back, leaving Mother in the
                    car.

MOTHER: Like a dog.

STAN: You've got 'Five Live!' [*to* BERNICE] Then you come
            back and we'll take the rest.

BERNICE: And what will you be doing in the meantime?

STAN: Organizing things here. There are checks to be made
            – doors to be locked.

BERNICE: I wonder how you cope with it all sometimes. [*pick-
            ing up some bags*] Come on then, Mother.

MOTHER: Might as well put a collar and lead on me and have
            done with it!

                    [BERNICE *and* MOTHER *exit* S/L. STAN *sits on a bag,
                    looks out to sea, shivers at a cold wind and sighs.*
                    MARGARET *and* WILLIAM *enter* S/R, *arm in arm.*
                    They are both wrapped up against the cold.]

STAN: William and Margaret! Margaret and William!

WILLIAM: You make us sound like four people.

STAN: No, I'm just glad to catch you. We'll be off soon.

WILLIAM: Yes, we're all packed up as well. We've just had a last
            little toddle.

MARGARET: I think the weather's trying to tell us something.

STAN: Yes. 'Go home,' it's saying. 'Go home!'

MARGARET: Cup of tea, Stan? I've made up a Thermos.

STAN: No thanks all the same. If we cut out toilet breaks we
            can get back to Worcester Park in two and a half
            hours.

                    [MARGARET *goes into her hut.*]

            Do you ever get up Worcester Park way?

WILLIAM: Not really, no.

STAN: Only, if you ever do . . .

WILLIAM: Yes, of course.

[*He sits down as* MARGARET *comes out with two beakers of tea and sits down beside him.* STAN *takes a final bag from his hut. It clinks as he puts it down.*]

STAN: [*embarrassed*] Sparkling white wine empties.

[WILLIAM *and* MARGARET *say nothing.* STAN *locks the door of his hut then tests the lock.*]

It's always very final, isn't it, locking the old beach hut door?

MARGARET: A good holiday, though.

STAN: Oh, yes, apart from that business with the windbreak crowd – the week it rained every day – that wasp invasion and, of course, Pauline. I do apologize for Pauline.

MARGARET: What on earth for? She's had a lovely time. I've never seen such a change in a girl.

WILLIAM: I liked that bikini as well.

STAN: Oh, granted she's cheered up, but was it for the right reasons?

WILLIAM: You mean Doug?

STAN: Exactly. Is he a right reason?

WILLIAM: I rather like him.

MARGARET: Yes, I didn't think I was going to at first, but I've warmed to him. He's a very jolly chap – no pretensions.

STAN: Being jolly is all very well but . . .

MARGARET: But what?

STAN: Well, those nieces of his.

MARGARET: What about them?

STAN: Well, are they or aren't they?

MARGARET: Are they or aren't they what?

STAN: Well . . . you know.

WILLIAM: Oh, Stan, shame on you!

SAND CASTLES

MARGARET: They were only showing us some family photographs the other day. Their father is Doug's brother – looks rather like him.

STAN: Well, why don't they ever call Doug 'Uncle'?

MARGARET: I don't know. The modern way, I suppose.

STAN: I can't tell you what a weight off my mind this is.

WILLIAM: You seriously thought that Doug was romancing Pauline at the same time as . . . well, with two young girls?

STAN: The thought had crossed my mind, William, but no more than that. To tell you the truth, Bernice was the really suspicious one.

[*He jumps involuntarily as* BERNICE *enters* S/L.]

BERNICE: I've packed Mother and the bags.

STAN: Oh, good. I'll get the next load up.

[*He picks up some more bags, including the clinking one.*]

BERNICE: Mostly mineral water.

STAN: Oh, incidentally, William and Margaret have just confirmed that Debs and Becky really are Doug's nieces.

BERNICE: Oh. [*rallying*] Well, I never really thought anything else.

[*Feeling betrayed,* STAN *exits* S/L *with the bags.*]

MARGARET: You were never really suspicious then?

BERNICE: Oh, no. Stan was the really suspicious one. So, are you closing up today?

WILLIAM: Yes – a warm hearth beckons.

BERNICE: Incidentally, if you ever find yourselves in Worcester Park, don't be strangers.

WILLIAM: Oh, absolutely not.

BERNICE: Stan will give you one of his cards.

MARGARET: How kind.

[DEBS *and* BECKY *enter* S/R. *They are dressed for travelling.*]

DEBS: Oh, good, we caught you. We're just off.

BERNICE: With your uncle?

DEBS: No. Back home to Chelmsford. This time Monday I shall be doing shampoos and sets.

BECKY: Still, never mind. Italy next year.

DEBS: Ta-ta then, Bernice.

BECKY: Say goodbye to Stan for us.

BERNICE: Of course. If you're ever in Worcester Park . . .

BECKY: Oh, yes – right.

DEBS: Nice to have met you, Margaret.

MARGARET: Yes, you too – both of you.

BECKY: [*to* WILLIAM] And as for you!

DEBS: And as for you!

[*They each kiss* WILLIAM *on the cheek.*]

WILLIAM: Goodbye, my dears. Goodbye!

DEBS/BECKY: [*together*] Bye!

[*They exit* S/R, *waving. The others call out their goodbyes.*]

WILLIAM: Well, they may not have done the old blood pressure much good, but charming girls – charming.

[STAN *enters* S/L.]

STAN: Who's gone? Who were you saying goodbye to?

BERNICE: Doug's nieces.

STAN: Oh, right. He didn't go with them?

BERNICE: Of course not.

STAN: No, of course not. Well, Mother's getting restless so I suppose we'd best be making a move.

BERNICE: Haven't you forgotten something?

STAN: Nothing. I've been through my checklist twice.

BERNICE: What about Pauline?

STAN:	Oh. Well, what are the arrangements?
BERNICE:	I don't know.
STAN:	Well, is she at our hotel? Is she at Doug's hotel? Where's her case? Is she packed? This is a shambles!

[DOUG *enters* S/R.]

DOUG:	What's a shambles?
STAN:	Pauline!

[PAULINE *enters* S/R.]

PAULINE:	What?
DOUG:	Stan says you're a shambles.
PAULINE:	Oh, nice.
STAN:	I didn't mean you personally. I meant the arrangements.
PAULINE:	Well, I am arranged. I'm all packed and ready to go.
STAN:	You could have told me.
PAULINE:	I just have.
BERNICE:	Only, Mother's getting restless in the Range Rover.
DOUG:	Shall I pop up and calm her down?
BERNICE:	No thank you.
DOUG:	Fair enough. Well, that looks like it then.
STAN:	Look, Doug. I hate to wave the big stick at you, but what about your hut?
DOUG:	Oh, I'm not taking that with me.
STAN:	I meant the contents. You're not like us – you're not permanent. You're a renter. You can't just leave stuff in there till next year.
DOUG:	I haven't. We packed up last night.
STAN:	Including the dinghy?
DOUG:	No. I couldn't deflate it so I gave it to some kids.
STAN:	You'll need to give the key back.
DOUG:	I'll do that on my way past the shop.
STAN:	Well, I must admit you seem very organized.

DOUG: It's probably something I've picked up from you, Stan.

STAN: [*flattered*] Really?

BERNICE: Shall we see you next year then?

DOUG: Highly unlikely, Bernice. I seldom go to the same place twice. It all gets a bit samey.

BERNICE: [*defensively*] Stan and I went to Amsterdam at Easter.

DOUG: Oh. Well, good.

WILLIAM: I suppose Margaret and I have got 'samey' over the years.

MARGARET: Mr. and Mrs. Samey.

STAN: Not that there's anything wrong with that. It's not a sin!

DOUG: Whatever takes your fancy, Stan.

BERNICE: You hated Amsterdam anyway.

STAN: Not 'hated'. I just didn't get on with it. [*to* DOUG] Of course, you realize you've created a problem.

DOUG: I'm sorry to hear that. I know I may have ruffled a few feathers but . . .

STAN: Not this year – next year.

DOUG: I've just told you, I'm not coming next year.

STAN: No, but somebody else will rent the hut. We'll have new renters to cope with!

DOUG: Look on the bright side, Stan. They might learn those unwritten rules of yours in five minutes. You might not even need to get your flowerpots out.

STAN: [*unsure*] Mmm.

DOUG: Anyway, time for the off. [*shaking hands*] William, Margaret – it's been a pleasure.

MARGARET: Yes, it has.

WILLIAM: Goodbye, Doug. Keep the batter up to scratch.

PAULINE: [*kissing* MARGARET*'s cheek*] Goodbye, Margaret.

MARGARET: You stay happy now.

PAULINE: I'll do my best. Goodbye, William.

WILLIAM: Goodbye, my dear.

                       [PAULINE *kisses his cheek.*]

PAULINE: And you look after yourself.

WILLIAM: Oh, I am. I'm having a wonderful time being kissed
            by pretty girls.

STAN: Yes, well, kissing apart, Pauline, there is the matter
            of your case.

PAULINE: What about my case?

STAN: I'd like to know its whereabouts, that's all. I mean, it
            won't suddenly materialize in the Range Rover like
            Doctor Who's telephone box, will it?

PAULINE: It doesn't need to. It's in Doug's car.

STAN: And what use is that to me?

PAULINE: Think of it as information. Doug and I are leaving in
            his car together.

                       [BERNICE *puts her hands to her cheeks.*]

STAN: Where? Where?

DOUG: Well, you know they always say you need a holiday
            to get over a holiday? That's what we're going to have.

STAN: But the season's nearly over.

DOUG: Not in Portugal it isn't.

BERNICE: [*close to tears*] But . . . but . . .

                       [PAULINE *takes her by the shoulders.*]

PAULINE: Bernice, I'm not a child. I've got to dip my toe in the
            water again.

BERNICE: Well, if that's what you call it.

PAULINE: [*kissing her*] I'll be all right.

DOUG: Trust me. She'll be all right.

                       [*He kisses* BERNICE *and extends a hand to* STAN.]

            Cheers then, Stan.

STAN: Muted ones, I have to say.

PAULINE: Think of me as a load off your mind.

STAN: I'll try.

                  [PAULINE *kisses him on the cheek.*]

             And don't forget. If you and Doug are ever Worcester Park way . . .

PAULINE: Of course.

                  [DOUG *and* PAULINE *start to leave* S/R *but* STAN *stops them.*]

STAN: Doug?

DOUG: Yes, Stan?

STAN: [*gravely*] One last thing. Don't turn out to be a Rex Elphinstone, will you?

                  [*Quite naturally,* DOUG *hasn't the faintest idea what* STAN *means but decides to humour him and replies equally gravely.*]

DOUG: Stan, hand on heart, I'll try my best not to be.

                  [*He and* PAULINE *exit* S/R *while* WILLIAM *and* MARGARET *call out their goodbyes.* STAN *and* BERNICE *are rooted to the spot, stunned.* WILLIAM *and* MARGARET *lead them to the two remaining chairs and sit them down.*]

WILLIAM: What we really need is a St. Bernard with a barrel of brandy round its neck.

MARGARET: William!

WILLIAM: Sorry.

STAN: You are sure about the nieces really being nieces?

MARGARET: Quite sure, yes.

STAN: Thank heavens for small mercies, I suppose.

BERNICE: We've never been blessed with kiddies, you see, so Pauline – well, we've always kept an eye on her.

MARGARET: As she said, she's not a child.

WILLIAM: And I don't think anyone has Doug down as a white slaver.

BERNICE: No.

STAN: Do they still have those – white slavers?

MARGARET: William was being silly again.

BERNICE: So smile through the tears, eh?

WILLIAM: I don't think it's a time for tears at all. They seem very fond of each other.

STAN: It's just that Doug is – I don't know – off-centre somehow.

MARGARET: If it's any consolation, my mother thought that William was feckless.

BERNICE: Feckless? William is one of the most un-feckless people I know.

WILLIAM: I wore gaudy ties apparently.

STAN: Bernice's mother thought I was flashy because I drove a red convertible.

BERNICE: The rows I used to have with her.

MARGARET: Two hasty judgements, you see – wrong judgements – because all those years later, here we are and here you are.

BERNICE: We've never had a chance to talk like this before.

STAN: Do you know something? This makes me look forward to next year even more now.

[*A little pause before an answer.*]

WILLIAM: Oh, absolutely, yes.

[MOTHER *stamps on angrily* S/L.]

MOTHER: If you'd left the keys in the ignition I could have been home by now!

BERNICE: [*getting up*] Oh, Mother, I am sorry. We forgot all about you.

MOTHER: Dogs die in cars because people leave them there.

STAN: [*getting up*] Not in this weather, Mother.

MOTHER: And where's Pauline?

STAN: Now don't be shocked, but the thing is – they've sort of gone off together – her and Doug.

MOTHER: Oh. I thought they might.

> [*The others are surprised as to how easily she says this.*]

Well, are we going or do I have to get my chair out of the hut?

STAN: No, no. We're going.

> [*He shakes hands with* WILLIAM, *thinks about kissing* MARGARET *but decides against it and shakes her hand too.*]

William – Margaret – thanks for the pleasure of your company as always. *À bientôt,* as the French would have it.

WILLIAM: Cheerio, Stan.

MARGARET: Safe journey.

> [BERNICE *shakes their hands too.*]

BERNICE: Look forward to seeing you next year.

WILLIAM: Goodbye.

MARGARET: And don't worry about Pauline.

STAN: Say goodbye, Mother.

MOTHER: Oh, thanks for reminding me. I *was* going to say 'hello'. [*to* WILLIAM *and* MARGARET] Ta-ta then.

WILLIAM: Goodbye.

MARGARET: Goodbye, Mrs Billet.

> [MOTHER *leads the way off* S/L.]

MOTHER: And if you think we're getting home without a toilet break after the time I spent sitting in that armoured car of yours, you've got another think coming!

STAN: You never thought I was flashy with that red convertible, did you, Bernice?

BERNICE: I thought you were dead dashing.

STAN: [*loving this*] Dead dashing!

            [MOTHER, STAN *and* BERNICE *exit* S/L. WILLIAM
            and MARGARET *sit in their chairs.*]

MARGARET: Do you think you should have told them?

WILLIAM: About the time I was a white slaver?

MARGARET: You know very well what I mean. Next year.

WILLIAM: Doctors have been wrong before.

MARGARET: Of course they have.

WILLIAM: In any case, I couldn't lumber poor old Stan with the
            thought of *two* huts being rented.

MARGARET: He'd probably crack.

WILLIAM: I'm damned certain he would. Will you rent or will
            you sell it?

MARGARET: Don't be morbid.

WILLIAM: Just in case the quack was right.

MARGARET: You know that the ship's surgeon on the *Victory* diag-
            nosed Lord Nelson as having a slight flesh-wound?

WILLIAM: Are you sure about that?

MARGARET: Oh, it was all hushed up, of course.

            [*They both chuckle.*]

            Well, I suppose it's time we made a move.

WILLIAM: Where?

MARGARET: Home, of course. You said we were all packed up and
            ready to go.

WILLIAM: A little white lie. Actually, the forecast for next week
            is rather good. I thought we'd stay on for a bit.

MARGARET: What a good idea.

WILLIAM: I thought so. Think how lovely and peaceful it will
            be.

            [*They smile at each other and hold hands.*]

THE END